Tertullian
Ad Nationes

Tertullian
Ad Nationes

Tertullian
Ad Nationes

© Lighthouse Publishing 2015

All rights reserved. Without limiting the rights under copyright reserved above, no part of this publication may be reproduced, stored in a retrieval system, or transmitted, in any form or by any means (electronic, mechanical, photocopying, recording or otherwise), without the prior written permission of the copyright owner of this book.

Published by
Lighthouse Christian Publishing
SAN 257-4330
5531 Dufferin Drive
Savage, Minnesota, 55378
United States of America

www.lighthousechristianpublishing.com

Tertullian

Introductory Note.

[a.d. 145–220.] When our Lord repulsed the woman of Canaan (Matt. xv. 22) with apparent harshness, he applied to her people the epithet *dogs*, with which the children of Israel had thought it piety to reproach them. When He accepted her faith and caused it to be recorded for our learning, He did something more: He reversed the curse of the Canaanite and showed that the Church was designed "for all people;" Catholic alike for all time and for all sorts and conditions of men.

Thus the North-African Church was loved before it was born: the Good Shepherd was gently leading those "that were with young." Here was the charter of those Christians to be a Church, who then were Canaanites in the land of their father Ham. It is remarkable indeed that among these pilgrims and strangers to the West the first elements of Latin Christianity come into view. Even at the close of the Second Century the Church in Rome is an inconsiderable, though prominent, member of the great confederation of Christian Churches which has its chief seats in Alexandria and Antioch, and of which the entire Literature is Greek. It is an African presbyter who takes from Latin Christendom the reproach of theological and literary barrenness and begins the great work in which, upon his foundations, Cyprian and Augustine built up, with incomparable genius, that Carthaginian School of Christian thought by which Latin Theology was dominated for centuries. It is important to note (1.) that providentially not one of these illustrious doctors died in Communion with the Roman See, pure though it was and venerable at that time; and (2.) that to the works of Augustine the Reformation in Germany and Continental Europe was largely due; while (3.) the *specialties* of the Anglican Reformation were, in like proportion, due to the writings of Tertullian and Cyprian. The hinges of great and controlling destinies for Western Europe and our own America are to be found in the period we are now approaching.

The merest school-boy knows much of the history of Carthage, and how the North Africans became Roman citizens. How they became Christians is not so clear. A melancholy destiny has enveloped Carthage from the outset, and its glory and greatness as a Christian See were transient indeed. It blazed out all at once in Tertullian, after about a century of missionary labours had been exerted upon its creation: and having given a Minucius Felix, an Arnobius and a Lactantius to adorn the earliest period of Western Ecclesiastical learning, in addition to its nobler luminaries, it rapidly declined. At the beginning of the Third Century, at a council presided over by Agrippinus, Bishop of Carthage, there were present not less than seventy bishops of the Province. A period of cruel persecutions followed, and the African Church received a baptism of blood.

Tertullian was born a heathen, and seems to have been educated at Rome, where he probably practiced as a jurisconsult. We may, perhaps, adopt most of the ideas of Allix, as conjecturally probable, and assign his birth to a.d. 145. He became a Christian about 185, and a presbyter about 190. The period of his strict orthodoxy very nearly expires with the century. He lived to an extreme old age, and some suppose even till a.d. 240. More probably we must adopt the date preferred by recent writers, a.d. 220.

It seems to be the fashion to treat of Tertullian as a Montanist, and only incidentally to celebrate his services to the Catholic Orthodoxy of Western Christendom. Were I his biographer I should reverse this course, as a mere act of justice, to say nothing of gratitude to a man of splendid intellect, to whom the filial spirit of Cyprian accorded the loving tribute of a disciple, and whose genius stamped itself upon the very words of Latin theology, and prepared the language for the labors of a Jerome. In creating the Vulgate, and so lifting the Western Churches into a position of intellectual equality with the East, the latter as well as St. Augustine himself were debtors to Tertullian in a degree not to be estimated by any other than the Providential Mind that inspired his brilliant career as a Christian.

In speaking of Tatian I laid the base for what I wished to say of Tertullian. Let God only be their judge; let us gratefully recognize the debt we owe to them. Let us read them, as we read the works of King Solomon. We must, indeed, approve of the discipline of the Primitive Age, which allowed of no compromises. The Church was struggling for existence, and could not permit any man to become her master. The more brilliant the intellect, the more dangerous to the poor Church were its perversions of her Testimony. Before the heathen tribunals, and in the market-places, it would not answer to let Christianity appear double tongued. The orthodoxy of the Church, not less than her children, was undergoing an ordeal of fire. It seems a miracle that her Testimony preserved its unity, and that heresy was branded as such by the instinct of the Faithful. Poor Tertullian was cut off by his own act. The weeping Church might bewail him as David mourned for Absalom, but like David, she could not give the Ark of God into other hands than those of the loyal and the true. I have set the writings of Tertullian in a natural and logical order, so as to aid the student, and to relieve him from the distractions of such an arrangement as one finds in Oehler's edition. Valuable as it is, the practical use of it is irritating and confusing. The reader of that edition may turn to the slightly differing schemes of Neander and Kaye, for a theoretical order of the works; but here he will find a classification which will aid his inquiries. He will find, first, those works which connect with the Apologists of the former volumes of this series: which illustrate the Church's position toward the outside world, the Jews as well as the Gentiles. Next come those works which contend with internal differences and heresies. And then, those which reflect the morals and manners of Christians. These are classed with some reference to their degrees of freedom from the Montanistic taint, and are followed, last of all, by the few tracts which belong to the melancholy period of his lapse, and are directed against the Church's orthodoxy.

Let it be borne in mind, that if this sad close of Tertullian's career cannot be extenuated, the later history of Latin Christianity forbids us to condemn him, in the tones which proceeded from the Virgin Church with authority, and which the law of her testimony and the instinct of self-preservation forced her to utter. Let us reflect that St. Bernard and after him the Schoolmen, whom we so deservedly honor, separated themselves far more absolutely than ever Tertullian did from the orthodoxy of Primitive Christendom. The schism which withdrew the West from Communion with the original seats of Christendom, and from Nicene Catholicity, was formidable beyond all expression, in comparison with Tertullian's entanglements with a delusion which the See of Rome itself had momentarily patronized. Since the Council of Trent, not a theologian of the Latins has been free from organic heresies, compared with which the fanaticism of our author was a trifling aberration. Since the late Council of the Vatican, essential Montanism has become organized in the Latin Churches: for what are the new revelations and oracles of the pontiff but the *deliria* of another claimant to the voice and inspiration of the Paraclete? Poor Tertullian! The sad influences of his decline and folly have been fatally felt in all the subsequent history of the West, but, surely subscribers to the Modern Creed of the Vatican have reason to "speak gently of *their father's* fall." To Döllinger, with the "Old Catholic" remnant only, is left the right to name the Montanists heretics, or to upbraid Tertullian as a lapser from Catholicity.

From Dr. Holmes, I append the following Introductory Notice:

(I.) Quintus Septimius Florens Tertullianus, as our author is called in the mss. of his works, is thus noticed by Jerome in his *Catalogus Scriptorum Ecclesiasticorum:* "Tertullian, a presbyter, the first Latin writer after Victor and Apollonius, was a native of the province of Africa and city of Carthage, the son of a proconsular centurion: he was a man of a sharp and vehement temper, flourished under Severus and Antoninus Caracalla, and wrote numerous works, which (as they are generally known) I think it unnecessary to particularize. I saw at Concordia, in Italy, an old man named Paulus. He said that when young he had met at Rome with an aged amanuensis of the blessed Cyprian, who told him that Cyprian never passed a day without reading some portion of Tertullian's works, and used frequently to say, *Give me my master*, meaning Tertullian. After remaining a presbyter of the church until he had attained the middle age of life, Tertullian was, by the envy and contumelious treatment of the Roman clergy, driven to embrace the opinions of Montanus, which he has mentioned in several of his works under the title of the New Prophecy....He is reported to have lived to a very advanced age, and to have composed many other works which are not extant." We add Bishop Kaye's notes on this extract, in an abridged shape: "The correctness of some parts of this account has been questioned. Doubts have been entertained whether Tertullian was a presbyter, although these have solely arisen from Roman Catholic objections to a married priesthood; for it is certain that he was married, there being among his works two treatises addressed to his wife....Another question has been raised respecting the place where Tertullian officiated as a presbyter—whether at Carthage or at Rome. That he at one time resided at Carthage may be inferred from Jerome's statement, and is rendered certain by several passages of his own writings. Allix supposes that the notion of his having been a presbyter of the Roman Church owed its rise to what Jerome said of the envy and abuse of the Roman clergy impelling him to espouse the party of Montanus. Optatus, and the author of the work *de Hæresibus*, which Sirmond edited under the title of Prædestinatus, expressly call him a Carthaginian presbyter. Semler, however, in a dissertation inserted in his edition of Tertullian's works, contends that he was a presbyter of the Roman Church. Eusebius tells us that he was accurately acquainted with the Roman laws, and on other accounts a distinguished person at Rome. Tertullian displays, moreover, a knowledge of the proceedings of the Roman Church with respect to Marcion and Valentinus, who were once members of it, which could scarcely have been obtained by one who had not himself been numbered amongst its presbyters Semler admits that, after Tertullian seceded from the church, he left and returned to Carthage. Jerome does not inform us whether Tertullian was born of Christian parents, or was converted to Christianity. There are passages in his writings which seem to imply that he had been a Gentile; yet he may perhaps mean to describe, not his own condition, but that of Gentiles in general, before their conversion. Allix and the majority of commentators understand them literally, as well as some other passages in which he speaks of his own infirmities and sinfulness. His writings show that he flourished at the period specified by Jerome—that is, during the reigns of Severus and Antoninus Caracalla, or between the years a.d. 193 and 216; but they supply no precise information respecting the date of his birth, or any of the principal occurrences of his life. Allix places his birth about 145 or 150; his conversion to Christianity about a.d. 185; his marriage about 186; his admission to the priesthood about 192; his adoption of the opinions of Montanus about 199; and his death about a.d. 220.

But these dates, it must be understood, rest entirely on conjecture."

(II.) Tertullian's work against Marcion, as it happens, is, *as to its date*, the best authenticated—perhaps the only well authenticated—particular connected with the author's life. He himself mentions the fifteenth year of the reign of Severus as the time when he was writing the work: "Ad xv. jam Severi imperatoris." This agrees with Jerome's Chronicle, where occurs this note: "Anno 2223 Severi xv^{o} Tertullianus...celebratur." This year is assigned to the year of our Lord 207; but notwithstanding the certainty of this date, it is far from clear that it describes more than the time of the publication of *the first book*. On the contrary, it is nearly certain that the other books, although connected manifestly enough in the author's argument and purpose (compare the initial and the final chapters of the several books), were yet issued at separate times. Noesselt shows that between the Book i. and Books ii.-iv. Tertullian issued his *De Præscript. Hæret.*, and previous to Book v. he published his tracts, *De Carne Christi* and *De Resurrectione Carnis*. After giving the incontestable date of the xv. of Severus for the first book, he says it is a mistake to suppose that the other books were published with it. He adds: "Although we cannot undertake to determine whether Tertullian issued his Books ii., iii., iv., against Marcion, together or separately, or in what year, we yet venture to affirm that Book v. appeared apart from the rest. For the tract *De Resurr. Carnis* appears from its second chapter to have been published after the tract *De Carne Christi*, in which latter work (chap. vii.) he quotes a passage from the fourth book against Marcion. But in his Book v. against Marcion (chap. x.), he refers to his work *De Resurr. Carnis*; which circumstance makes it evident that Tertullian published his Book v. at a different time from his Book iv. In his Book i. he announces his intention (chap. i.) of some time or other completing his tract *De Præscript. Hæret.*, but in his book *De Carne Christi* (chap. ii.), he mentions how he had completed it,—a conclusive proof that his Book i. against Marcion preceded the other books."

(III.) Respecting Marcion himself, the most formidable heretic who had as yet opposed revealed truth, enough will turn up in this treatise, with the notes which we have added in explanation, to satisfy the reader. It will, however, be convenient to give here a few introductory particulars of him. Tertullian mentions Marcion as being, with Valentinus, in communion with the Church at Rome, "under the episcopate of the blessed Eleutherus." He goes on to charge them with "ever-restless curiosity, with which they infected even the brethren;" and informs us that they were more than once put out of communion—"Marcion, indeed, with the 200 sesterces which he brought into the church." He goes on to say, that "being at last condemned to the banishment of a perpetual separation, they sowed abroad the poisons of their doctrines. Afterwards, when Marcion, having professed penitence, agreed to the terms offered to him, that he should receive reconciliation on condition that he brought back to the church the rest also, whom he had trained up for perdition, he was prevented by death." He was a native of Sinope in Pontus, of which city, according to an account preserved by Epiphanius, which, however, is somewhat doubtful, his father was bishop, and of high character both for his orthodoxy and exemplary practice. He came to Rome soon after the death of Hyginus, probably about a.d. 141 or 142; and soon after his arrival he adopted the heresy of Cerdon.

(IV.) It is an interesting question as to what edition of the Holy Scriptures Tertullian used in his very copious quotations. It may at once be asserted that he did not cite from the Hebrew, although some writers have claimed for him, among his varied learning, a knowledge of the sacred language. Bp. Kaye observes, page 61, n. 1, that "he sometimes speaks as if he was acquainted with Hebrew," and refers to the *Anti-Marcion* iv. 39, the *Adv. Praxeam* v., and the *Adv. Judæos* ix. Be this as it may, it is manifest that Tertullian's Scripture passages never resemble the Hebrew, but in nearly every instance the Septuagint, whenever, as is most frequently the case, that version differs from the original. In the New Testament there is, as might be expected, a tolerably close conformity to the Greek. There is, however, it must be allowed, a sufficiently frequent variation from the letter of both the Greek Testaments to justify Semler's suspicion that Tertullian always quoted from the old Latin version, whatever that might have been, which was current in the African church in the second and third centuries. The most valuable part of Semler's *Dissertatio de varia et incerta indole Librorum Q. S. F. Tertulliani* is his investigation of this very point. In section iv. he endeavors to prove this proposition: "Hic scriptor non in manibus habuit Græcos libros sacros;" and he states his conclusion thus: "Certissimum est nec Tertullianum nec Cyprianum nec ullum scriptorem e Latinis illis ecclesiasticis provocare unquam ad Græcorum librorum auctoritatem si vel maxime obscura aut contraria lectio occurreret;" and again: "Ex his satis certum est, Latinos satis diu secutos fuisse auctoritatem suorum librorum adversus Græcos, nec concessisse nisi serius, cum Augustini et Hieronymi nova auctoritas juvare videretur." It is not ignorance of Greek which is imputed to Tertullian, for he is said to have well understood that language, and even to have composed in it. He probably followed the Latin, as writers now usually quote the authorized English, as being current and best known among their readers. Independent feeling, also, would have weight with such a temper as Tertullian's, to say nothing of the suspicion which largely prevailed in the African branch of the Latin church, that the Greek copies of the Scriptures were much corrupted by the heretics, who were chiefly, if not wholly, Greeks or Greek-speaking persons.

(V.) Whatever perverting effect Tertullian's secession to the sect of Montanus may have had on his judgment in his latest writings, it did not vitiate the work against Marcion. With a few trivial exceptions, this treatise may be read by the strictest Catholic without any feeling of annoyance. His lapse to Montanism is set down conjecturally as having taken place a.d. 199. Jerome, we have seen, attributed the event to his quarrel with the Roman clergy, but this is at least doubtful; nor must it be forgotten that Tertullian's mind seems to have been peculiarly suited by nature to adopt the mystical notions and ascetic principles of Montanus. It is satisfactory to find that, on the whole, "the authority of Tertullian," as the learned Dr. Burton says, "upon great points of doctrine is considered to be little, if at all, affected by his becoming a Montanist." (*Lectures on Eccl. Hist.* vol. ii. p. 234.) Besides the different works which are expressly mentioned in the notes of this volume, recourse has been had by the translator to Dupin's *Hist. Eccl. Writers* (trans.), vol. i. pp. 69-86; Tillemont's *Mèmoires Hist. Eccl.* iii. 85-103; Dr. Smith's *Greek and Roman Biography*, articles "Marcion" and "Tertullian;" Schaff's article, in Herzog's *Cyclopædia*, on "Tertullian;" Munter's *Primordia Eccl. Africanæ*, pp. 118-150; Robertson's *Church Hist.* vol. i. pp. 70-77; Dr. P. Schaff's *Hist. of Christian Church* (New York, 1859, pp. 511-519), and Archdeacon Evans' *Biography of the Early Church*, vol. i. (Lives of "Marcion," pp. 93-122, and "Tertullian," pp. 325-363). This last work, though of a popular cast, shows a good deal of research and learning, expressed in the pleasant style of the once popular author of *The Rectory of Vale Head*. The translator has mentioned these works, because they are all quite accessible to the general reader, and will give him adequate information concerning the subject treated in the present volume.

To this introduction of Dr. Holmes must be added that of Mr. Thelwall, the translator of the Third volume in the Edinburgh Series, as follows:

> To arrange chronologically the works (especially if numerous) of an author whose own date is known with tolerable precision, is not always or necessarily easy: witness the controversies as to the succession of St. Paul's epistles. To

do this in the case of an author whose own date is itself a matter of controversy may therefore be reasonably expected to be still less so; and such is the predicament of him who attempts to perform this task for Tertullian. I propose to give a specimen or two of the difficulties with which the task is beset; and then to lay before the reader briefly a summary of the results at which eminent scholars, who have devoted much time and thought to the subject, have arrived. Such a course, I think, will at once afford him means of judging of the absolute impossibility of arriving at definite certainty in the matter; and induce him to excuse me if I prefer furnishing him with materials from which to deduce his own conclusions, rather than venturing on an *ex cathedra* decision on so doubtful a subject.

I. The book, as Dr. Holmes has reminded us, of the date of which we seem to have the surest evidence, is *Adv. Marc.* i. This book was in course of writing, as its author himself (c. 15) tells us, "in the fifteenth year of the empire of Severus." Now this date would be clear if there were no doubt as to which year of our era corresponds to Tertullian's fifteenth of Severus. Pamelius, however, says Dr. Holmes, makes it a.d. 208; Clinton, (whose authority is more recent and better,) 207.

2. Another book which promises to give some clue to its date is the *de Pallio*. The writer uses these phrases: "præsentis imperii *triplex virtus;*" "Deo *tot Augustis in unum* favente;" which show that there were at the time three persons unitedly bearing the title *Augusti*—not *Cæsares* only, but the still higher *Augusti;*—while the remainder of that context, as well as the opening of c. 1, indicates a time of peace of some considerable duration; a time of plenty; and a time during and previous to which great changes had taken place in the general aspect of the Roman Empire, and some particular traitor had been discovered and frustrated. Such a combination of circumstances might seem to fix the date with some degree of assurance. But unhappily, as Kaye reminds us, commentators cannot agree as to who the three Augusti are. Some say

Severus, Caracalla, and *Albinus*; some say Severus, Caracalla, and *Geta*. Hence we have a difference of some twelve years or thereabouts in the computations. For Albinus was defeated by Severus in person, and fell by his own hand, in a.d. 197; and Geta, Severus' second son, brother of Caracalla, was not associated by his father with himself and his other son as *Augustus* until a.d. 208, though he had received the title of *Cæsar* ten years before, in the same year in which *Caracalla* had received that of Augustus. For my own part, I may perhaps be allowed to say that I should incline to agree, like Salmasius, with those who assign the later date. The limits of the present Introduction forbid my entering at large into my reasons for so doing. I am, however, supported in it by the authority of Neander. In one point, though, I should hesitate to agree with Oehler, who appears to follow Salmasius and others herein,— namely, in understanding the expression "et cacto et rubo subdolæ familiaritatis convulso" of *Albinus*. It seems to me the words might with more propriety be applied to *Plautianus*; and that in the word "familiaritatis" we may see (after Tertullian's fashion) a play upon the meaning, with a reference not only to the long-standing but mischievous *intimacy* which existed between Severus and his countryman (perhaps fellow-townsman) Plautianus, who for his harshness and cruelty is fitly compared to the prickly *cactus*. He alludes likewise to the alliance which this ambitious prætorian præfect had contrived to contract with the *family* of the emperor, by the marriage of his daughter Plautilla to Caracalla,—an event which, as it turned out, led to his own death. Thus in the *"rubo"* there may be a reference to the ambitious and conceited "bramble" of Jotham's parable, and perhaps, too, to the "thistle" of Jehoash's. If this be so, the date would be at least approximately fixed, as Plautianus did not marry his daughter to Caracalla till a.d. 203, and was himself put to death in the following year, 204, while Geta, as we have seen, was made Augustus in 208.

3. The date of the *Apology*, however, is perhaps at once the most contested, and the most strikingly illustrative of the difficulties to which allusion has been made. It is not surprising that its date *should* have been more disputed than that of other pieces, inasmuch as it is the best known, and (for some reasons) the most interesting and famous, of all our author's productions. In fact, the dates assigned to it by different authorities vary from Mosheim's 198 to that suggested by the very learned Allix, who assigns it to 217.

4. Once more. In the tract *de Monogamia* (c. 3) the author says that since the date of St. Paul's first Epistle to the Corinthians "about 160 years had elapsed." Here, again, did we only know with certainty the precise date of that epistle, we could ascertain "about" the date of the tract. But (a) the date of the epistle is itself variously given, Burton giving it as early as a.d. 52, Michaelis and Mill as late as 57; and (b) Tertullian only says, "Armis *circiter* clx. exinde productis;" while the way in which, in the *ad Natt.*, within the short space of three chapters, he states first that 250, and then (in c. 9) that 300, years had not elapsed since the rise of the Christian name, leads us to think that here again he only desires to speak in round numbers, meaning perhaps *more* than 150, but *less* than 170.

These specimens must suffice, though it might be easy to add to them. There is, however, another classification of our author's writings which has been attempted. Finding the haplessness of strict chronological accuracy, commentators have seized on the idea that peradventure there might be found at all events some internal marks by which to determine which of them were written before, which after, the writer's secession to Montanism. It may be confessed that this attempt has been somewhat more successful than the other. Yet even here there are two formidable obstacles standing in our way. The first and greatest is, that the natural temper of Tertullian was from the first so akin to the spirit of Montanism, that, unless there occur distinct allusions to the "New Prophecy," or expressions specially connected with Montanistic phraseology, the *general tone* of any treatise is not a very safe guide. The second is, that the subject-matter of some of the treatises is not such as to afford much scope for the introduction of the peculiarities of a sect which professed to differ in discipline only, not doctrine, from the church at large.

Still the result of this classification seems to show one important feature of agreement between commentators, however they may differ upon details; and that is, that considerably the larger part of our author's rather voluminous productions must have been subsequent to his lamented secession. I think the best way to give the reader means for forming his own judgment will be, as I have said, to lay before him in parallel columns a tabular view of the disposition of the books by Dr. Neander and Bishop Kaye. These two modern writers, having given particular care to the subject, bringing to bear upon it all the advantages derived from wide reading, eminent abilities, and a diligent study of the works of preceding writers on the same questions, have a special right to be heard upon the matter in hand; and I think, if I may be allowed to say so, that, for calm judgment, and minute acquaintance with his author, I shall not be accused of undue partiality if I express my opinion that, as far as my own observation goes, the palm must be awarded to the Bishop. In this view I am supported by the fact that the accomplished Professor Ramsay, follows Dr. Kaye's arrangement. I premise that Dr. Neander adopts a threefold division, into:

    1. Writings which were occasioned by the relation of the Christians to the heathen, and refer to their vindication of Christianity against the heathen; attacks on heathenism; the sufferings and conduct of Christians under persecution; and the intercourse of Christians with heathens:

    2. Writings which relate to Christian and church life, and to ecclesiastical discipline:

    3. The dogmatic and dogmatico-controversial treatises. And under each head he subdivides into:

a. Pre-Montanist writings; b. Post-Montanist writings: thus leaving no room for what Kaye calls "works respecting which nothing certain can be pronounced." For the sake of clearness, this order has not been followed in the table. On the other side, it will be seen that Dr. Kaye, while not assuming to speak with more than a reasonable probability, is careful so to arrange the treatises under each head as to show the order, so far as it is discoverable, in which the books under that head were published; i.e., if one book is quoted in another book, the book so quoted, if distinctly referred to as already before the world, is plainly anterior to that in which it is quoted. Thus, then, have:

Neander.
I. *Pre-Montanist.*
1. De Poenitentia.
2. De Oratione.
3. De Baptismo.
4. Ad Uxorem i.
5. Ad Uxorem ii.
6. Ad Martyres.
7. De Patientia.
8. De Spectaculis.
9. De Idololatria.
10. 11. Ad Nationes i. ii.
12. Apologeticus.
13. De Testimonio Animæ.
14. De Præscr. Hæreticorum.
15. De Cult. Fem. i.
16. De Cult. Fem. ii.
II. *Montanist.*
17–21. Adv. Marc. i. ii. iii. iv. v.
22. De Anima.
23. De Carne Christi.
24. De Res. Carn.
25. De Cor. Mil.

26. De Virg. Vel.
27. De Ex. Cast.
28. De Monog.
29. De Jejuniis.
30. De Pudicitia.
31. De Pallio.
32. Scorpiace.
33. Ad Scapulam.
34. Adv. Valentinianos.
35. Adv. Hermogenem.
36. Adv. Praxeam.
37. Adv. Judæos.
38. De Fuga in Persecutione.
Kaye.
I. *Pre-Montanist* (probably).
1. De Poenitentia.
2. De Oratione.
3. De Baptismo.
4. Ad Uxorem i.
5. Ad Uxorem ii.
6. Ad Martyres.
7. De Patientia.
8. Adv. Judæos.
9. De Præscr. Hæreticorum.
II. *Montanist* (certainly).
10. Adv. Marc. i.
11. Adv. Marc. ii.
12. De Anima.
13. Adv. Marc. iii.
14. Adv. Marc. iv.
15. De Carne Christi.
16. De Resurrectione Carnis.
17. Adv. Marc. v.
18. Adv. Praxeam.
19. Scorpiace.
20. De Corona Militis.

21. De Virginibus Velandis.
22. De Exhortatione Castitatis.
23. De Fuga in Persecutione.
24. De Monogamia.
25. De Jejuniis.
26. De Pudicitia.
III. *Montanist* (probably).
27. Adv. Valentinianos.
28. Ad Scapulam.
29. De Spectaculis.
30. De Idololatria.
31. De Cultu Feminarum i.
32. De Cultu Feminarum ii.
IV. *Works respecting which nothing certain can be pronounced.*
33. The Apology.
34. Ad Nationes i.
35. Ad Nationes ii.
36. De Testimonio Animæ.
37. De Pallio.
38. Adv. Hermogenem.

A comparison of these two lists will show that the difference between the two great authorities is, as Kaye remarks, "not great; and with respect to some of the tracts on which we differ, the learned author expresses himself with great diffidence." The main difference, in fact, is that which affects two tracts upon kindred subjects, the *de Spectaculis*, and *Idololatria*, the *de Cultu Feminarum* (a subject akin to the other two), and the *adv. Judæos*. With reference to all these, except the last, to which I believe the Archdeacon does not once refer, the Bishop's opinion appears to have the support of Archdeacon Evans, whose learned and interesting essay, referred to in the note, appears in a volume published in 1837. Dr. Kaye's Lectures, on which his book is founded, were delivered in 1825. Of the date of his first edition I am not aware. Dr. Neander's *Antignostikus* also first appeared in 1825.

The preface to his second edition bears date July 1, 1849. As to the *adv. Judæos*, I confess I agree with Neander in thinking that, at all events from the beginning of c. 9, it is spurious. If it be urged that Jerome expressly quotes it as Tertullian's, I reply, Jerome so quotes it, I believe, when he is expounding *Daniel*. Now all that the *adv. Jud.* has to say about *Daniel* ends with the end of c. 8. It is therefore quite compatible with the fact thus stated to recognize the earlier half of the book as genuine, and to reject the rest, beginning, as it happens, just after the eighth chapter, as spurious. Perhaps Dr. Neander's Jewish birth and training peculiarly fit him to be heard on this question. Nor do I think Professor Ramsay (in the article above alluded to) has quite seen the force of Kaye's own remarks on Neander. What he does say is equally creditable to his candor and his accuracy; namely: "The instances alleged by Dr. Neander, in proof of this position, are undoubtedly very remarkable; but if the concluding chapters of the tract are spurious, no ground seems to be left for asserting that the genuine portion was posterior to the third Book against Marcion,—and none, consequently, for asserting that it was written by a Montanist." With which remark I must draw these observations on the genuine extant works of Tertullian to a close.

The next point to which a brief reference must be made is the *lost works* of Tertullian, lists of these are given both by Oehler and by Kaye, viz.:

1. A Book on Aaron's Robes: mentioned by Jerome, Epist. 128, *ad Fabiolam de Veste Sacerdotali* (tom. ii. p. 586, Opp. ed. Bened.).

2. A Book on the Superstition of the Age.

3. A Book on the Submission of the Soul.

4. A Book on the Flesh and the Soul.

Nos. 2, 3, and 4 are known only by their titles, which are found in the Index to Tertullian's works given in the *Codex Agobardi*; but the tracts themselves are not extant in the ms., which appears to have once contained—

5. A Book on Paradise, named in the Index, and referred to in *de Anima* 55, *adv. Marc.* iii. 12; and

6. A Book on the Hope of the Faithful: also named in the Index, and referred to *adv. Marc.* iii. 24; and by Jerome in his account of Papias, and on Ezek. xxxvi.; and by Gennadius of Marseilles.

7. Six Books on Ecstasy, with a seventh in reply to Apollonius: see Jerome. See, too, J. A. Fabricius on the words of the unknown author whom the Jesuit Sirmond edited under the name *Prœdestinatus*; who gathers thence that "Soter, pope of the City, and Apollonius, bishop of the Ephesians, wrote a book against the Montanists; *in reply to whom* Tertullian, a Carthaginian presbyter, wrote." J. Pamelius thinks these seven books were originally published *in Greek*.

8. A Book in reply to the Apellesites (i.e. the followers of Apelles): referred to in *de Carne Christi*, c. 8.

9. A Book on the Origin of the Soul, in reply to Hermogenes: referred to in *de Anima*, cc. 1, 3, 22, 24.

10. A Book on Fate: referred to by Fulgentius Planciades, p. 562, Merc.; also referred to as either written, or intended to be written, by Tertullian himself, *de Anima*, c. 20. Jerome states that there was extant, or had been extant, a book on Fate under the name of Minucius Felix, written indeed by a perspicuous author, but not in the style of Minucius Felix. This, Pamelius judged, should perhaps be rather ascribed to Tertullian.

11. A Book on the Trinity. Jerome says: "Novatian wrote....a large volume on the Trinity, *as if making an epitome of a work of Tertullian's, which most men not knowing regard it as Cyprian's.*" Novatian's book stood in Tertullian's name in the mss. of J. Gangneius, who was the first to edit it; in a Malmesbury ms. which Sig. Gelenius used; and in others.

12. A Book addressed to a Philosophic Friend on the Straits of Matrimony. Both Kaye and Oehler are in doubt whether Jerome's words, by which some have been led to conclude that Tertullian wrote some book or books on this and kindred subjects, really imply as much, or whether they may

not refer merely to those tracts and passages in his extant writings which touch upon such matters. Kaye hesitates to think that the "Book to a Philosophic Friend" is the same as the *de Exhortatione Castitatis*, because Jerome says Tertullian wrote on the subject of celibacy *"in his youth;"* but as Cave takes what Jerome elsewhere says of Tertullian's leaving the Church *"about the middle of his age"* to mean his *spiritual age*, the same sense might attach to his words here too, and thus obviate the Bishop's difficulty.

There are some other works which have been attributed to Tertullian—on Circumcision; on Animals Clean and Unclean; on the truth that God is a Judge—which Oehler likewise rejects, believing that the expressions of Jerome refer only to passages in the *Anti-Marcion* and other extant works. To Novatian Jerome does ascribe a distinct work on Circumcision, and this may (comp. 11, just above) have given rise to the view that Tertullian had written one also.

There were, moreover, three treatises at least written by Tertullian *in Greek*. They are:

1. A Book on Public Shows. See *de Cor.* c. 6.
2. A Book on Baptism. See *de Bapt.* c. 15.
3. A Book on the Veiling of Virgins. See de *V. V.* c. 1.

Oehler adds that J. Pamelius, in his epistle dedicatory to Philip II. of Spain, makes mention of a *Greek copy* of Tertullian in the library of that king. This report, however, since nothing has ever been seen or heard of the said copy from that time, Oehler judges to be erroneous.

It remains briefly to notice the confessedly spurious works which the editions of Tertullian generally have appended to them. With these Kaye does not deal. The fragment, *adv. omnes Hæreses*, Oehler attributes to Victorinus Petavionensis, i.e., Victorinus bishop of Pettaw, on the Drave, in Austrian Styria. It was once thought he ought to be called *Pictaviensis*, i.e. of *Poictiers*; but John Launoy has shown this to be an error. Victorinus is said by Jerome to have "understood Greek better than Latin; hence his works are excellent for the sense, but mean as to the style." Cave believes him to have been a Greek by birth. Cassiodorus states him to have been once a professor of rhetoric. Jerome's statement agrees with the style of the tract in question; and Jerome distinctly says Victorinus did write *adversus omnes Hæreses*. Allix leaves the question of its authorship quite uncertain. If Victorinus be the author, the book falls clearly within the Ante-Nicene period; for Victorinus fell a martyr in the Diocletian persecution, probably about a.d. 303.

The next fragment—"Of the Execrable Gods of the Heathens"—is of quite uncertain authorship. Oehler would attribute it "to some declaimer not quite ignorant of Tertullian's writings," but certainly not to Tertullian himself.

Lastly we come to the metrical fragments. Concerning these, it is perhaps impossible to assign them to their rightful owners. Oehler has not troubled himself much about them; but he seems to regard the *Jonah* as worthy of more regard than the rest, for he seems to have intended giving more labor to its editing at some future time. Whether he has ever done so, or given us his German version of Tertullian's own works, which, "si Deus adjuverit," he distinctly promises in his preface, I do not know. Perhaps the best thing to be done under the circumstances is to give the judgment of the learned Peter Allix. It may be premised that by the celebrated George Fabricius—who published his great work, *Poetarum Veterum Ecclesiasticorum Opera Christiana*, etc., in 1564—the *Five Books in Reply to Marcion*, and the *Judgment of the Lord*, are ascribed to Tertullian, the *Genesis* and *Sodom* to Cyprian. Pamelius likewise seems to have ascribed the *Five Books*, the *Jonah*, and the *Sodom* to Tertullian; and according to Lardner, Bishop Bull likewise attributed the *Five Books* to him. They have been generally ascribed to the Victorinus above mentioned. Tillemont, among others, thinks they may well enough be his. Rigaltius is content to demonstrate that they are not Tertullian's, but leaves the real authorship without attempting to decide it. Of the others the same eminent critic says, "They seem to have been written at Carthage, at an age not far removed from Tertullian's." Allix, after observing that Pamelius is inconsistent with himself in attributing the *Genesis* and *Sodom* at one time to Tertullian, at another to Cyprian, rejects both views equally, and assigns the Genesis with some confidence to Salvian, a presbyter of Marseilles, whose "floruit" Cave gives *cir.* 440, a contemporary of Gennadius, and a copious author. To this it is, Allix thinks, that Gennadius alludes in his *Catalogue of Illustrious Men*, c. 77.

The *Judgment of the Lord* Allix ascribes to one Verecundus, an African bishop, whose date he finds it difficult to decide exactly. He refers to two of the name: one Bishop of Tunis, whom Victor of Tunis in his chronicle mentions as having died in exile at Chalcedon a.d. 552; the other Bishop of Noba, who visited Carthage with many others a.d. 482, at the summons of King Huneric, to answer there for their faith;— and would ascribe the poem to the former, thinking that he finds an allusion to it in the article upon that Verecundus in the *de Viris Illustribus* of Isidore of Seville. Oehler agrees with him. The *Five Books* Allix seems to hint may be attributed to some imitator of the Victorinus of Pettaw named above. Oehler attributes them rather to one Victorinus, or Victor, of Marseilles, a rhetorician, who died a.d. 450. He appears in G. Fabricius as Claudius Marius Victorinus, writer of a *Commentary on Genesis*, and an epistle *ad Salomonem Abbata*, both in verse, and of some considerable length.

Ad Nationes.
Book I.

Chapter I.—The Hatred Felt by the Heathen Against the Christians is Unjust, Because Based on Culpable Ignorance. One proof of that ignorance of yours, which condemns whilst it excuses your injustice, is at once apparent in the fact, that all who once shared in your ignorance and hatred (of the Christian religion), as soon as they have come to know it, leave off their hatred when they cease to be ignorant; nay more, they actually themselves become what they had hated, and take to hating what they had once been. Day after day, indeed, you groan over the increasing number of the Christians. Your constant cry is, that the state is beset (by us); that Christians are in your fields, in your camps, in your islands. You grieve over it as a calamity, that each sex, every age—in short, every rank—is passing over from you to us; yet you do not even after this set your minds upon reflecting whether there be not here some latent good. You do not allow yourselves in suspicions which may prove too true, nor do you like ventures which may be too near the mark. This is the only instance in which human curiosity grows torpid. You love to be ignorant of what other men rejoice to have discovered; you would rather not know it, because you now cherish your hatred as if you were aware that, (with the knowledge,) your hatred would certainly come to an end. Still, if there shall be no just ground for hatred, it will surely be found to be the best course to cease from the past injustice. Should, however, a cause have really existed there will be no diminution of the hatred, which will indeed accumulate so much the more in the consciousness of its justice; unless it be, forsooth, that you are ashamed to cast off your faults, or sorry to free yourselves from blame. I know very well with what answer you usually meet the argument from our rapid increase. That indeed must not, you say, be hastily accounted a good thing which converts a great number of persons, and gains them over to its side. I am aware how the mind is apt to take to evil courses. How many there are which forsake virtuous living! How many seek refuge in the opposite! Many, no doubt; nay, very many, as the last days approach. But such a comparison as this fails in fairness of application; for all are agreed in thinking thus of the evil-doer, so that not even the guilty themselves, who take the wrong side, and turn away from the pursuit of good to perverse ways, are bold enough to defend evil as good. Base things excite their fear, impious ones their shame. In short, they are eager for concealment, they shrink from publicity, they tremble when caught; when accused, they deny; even when tortured, they do not readily or invariably confess (their crime); at all events, they grieve when they are condemned. They reproach themselves for their past life; their change from innocence to an evil disposition they even attribute to fate. They cannot say that it is not a wrong thing, therefore they will not admit it to be their own act. As for the Christians, however, in what does their case resemble this? No one is ashamed; no one is sorry, except for his former (sins). If he is pointed at (for his religion), he glories in it; if dragged to trial, he does not resist; if accused, he makes no defense. When questioned, he confesses; when condemned, he rejoices. What sort of evil is this, in which the nature of evil comes to a standstill?

Chapter II.—The Heathen Perverted Judgment in the Trial of Christians. They Would Be More Consistent If They Dispensed with All Form of Trial. Tertullian Urges This with Much Indignation.

In this case you actually conduct trials contrary to the usual form of judicial process against criminals; for when culprits are brought up for trial, should they deny the charge, you press them for a confession by tortures. When Christians, however, confess without compulsion, you apply the torture to induce them to deny. What great perverseness is this, when you stand out against confession, *and* change the use of the torture, compelling the man who frankly acknowledges the charge to evade it, and him who is unwilling, to deny it? You, who preside for the purpose of extorting truth, demand falsehood from us alone that we may declare ourselves not to be what we are. I suppose you do not want us to be bad men, and therefore you earnestly wish to exclude us from that character. To be sure, you put others on the rack and the gibbet, to get them to deny what they have the reputation of being. Now, when they deny (the charge against them), you do not believe them but on our denial, you instantly believe us. If you feel sure that we are the most injurious of men, why, even in processes against us, are we dealt with by you differently from other offenders? I do not mean that you make no account of either an accusation or a denial (for your practice is not hastily to condemn men without an indictment and a defense); but, to take an instance in the trial of a murderer, the case is not at once ended, or the inquiry satisfied, on a man's confessing himself the murderer. However complete his confession, you do not readily believe him; but over and above this, you inquire into accessory circumstances—how often had he committed murder; with what weapons, in what place, with what plunder, accomplices, *and* abettors after the fact (was the crime perpetrated)—to the end that nothing whatever respecting the criminal might escape detection, and that every means should be at hand for arriving at a true verdict. In our case, on the contrary, whom you believe to be guilty of more atrocious and numerous crimes, you frame your indictments in briefer and lighter terms. I suppose you do not care to load with accusations men whom you earnestly wish to get rid of, or else you do not think it necessary to inquire into matters which are known to you already. It is, however, all the more perverse that you compel us to deny charges about which you have the clearest evidence. But, indeed, how much more consistent were it with your hatred of us to dispense with all forms of judicial process, and to strive with all your might not to urge us to say "No," and so have to acquit the objects of your hatred; but to confess all and singular the crimes laid to our charge, that your resentments might be the better glutted with an accumulation of our punishments, when it becomes known how many of those feasts each one of us may have celebrated, and how many incests we may have committed under cover of the night! What am I saying? Since your researches for rooting out our society must needs be made on a wide scale, you ought to extend your inquiry against our friends and companions. Let our infanticides and the dressers (of our horrible repasts) be brought out,—ay, and the very dogs which minister to our (incestuous) nuptials; then the business (of our trial) would be without a fault. Even to the crowds which throng the spectacles a zest would be given; for with how much greater eagerness would they resort to the theatre, when one had to fight in the lists who had devoured a hundred babies! For since such horrid and monstrous crimes are reported of us, they ought, of course, to be brought to light, lest they should seem to be incredible, and the public detestation of us should begin to cool. For most persons are slow to believe such things, feeling a horrible disgust at supposing that our nature could have an appetite for the food of wild beasts, when it has precluded these from all concubinage with the race of man.

Chapter III.—The Great Offence in the Christians Lies in Their Very Name. The Name Vindicated.

Since, therefore, you who are in other cases most scrupulous and persevering in investigating charges of far less serious import, relinquish your care in cases like ours, which are so horrible, and of such surpassing sin that *impiety* is too mild a word for them, by declining to hear confession, which should always be an important process for those who conduct judicial proceedings; and failing to make a full inquiry, which should be gone into by such as sue for a condemnation, it becomes evident that the crime laid to our charge consists not of any sinful conduct, but lies wholly in our *name*. If, indeed, any real crimes were clearly adducible against us, their very names would condemn us, if found applicable, so that distinct sentences would be pronounced against us in this wise: Let that murderer, or that incestuous criminal, or whatever it be that we are charged with, be led to execution, be crucified, or be thrown to the beasts. Your sentences, however, import only that one has confessed himself a Christian. No name of a crime stands against us, but only the crime of a name. Now this in very deed is neither more nor less than the entire odium which is felt against us. The name is the cause: some mysterious force intensified by your ignorance assails it, so that you do not wish to know for certain that which for certain you are sure you know nothing of; and therefore, further, you do not believe things which are not submitted to proof, and, lest they should be easily refuted, you refuse to make inquiry, so that the odious name is punished under the presumption of (real) crimes. In order, therefore, that the issue may be withdrawn from the offensive name, we are compelled to deny it; then upon our denial we are acquitted, with an entire absolution for the past: we are no longer murderers, no longer incestuous, because we have lost that name. But since this point is dealt with in a place of its own, do you tell us plainly why you are pursuing this name even to extirpation? What crime, what offence, what fault is there in a name? For you are barred by the rule which puts it out of your power to allege crimes (of any man), which no legal action moots, no indictment specifies, no sentence enumerates. In any case which is submitted to the judge, inquired into against the defendant, responded to by him or denied, and cited from the bench, I acknowledge a legal charge. Concerning, then, the merit of a name, whatever offence names may be charged with, whatever impeachment words may be amenable to, I for my part think, that not even a complaint is due to a word or a name, unless indeed it has a barbarous

Ad Nationes

sound, or smacks of ill-luck, or is immodest, or is indecorous for the speaker, or unpleasant to the hearer. These crimes in (mere) words and names are just like barbarous words and phrases, which have their fault, and their solecism, and their absurdity of figure. The name *Christian*, however, so far as its meaning goes, bears the sense of anointing. Even when by a faulty pronunciation you call us "Chrestians" (for you are not certain about even the sound of this noted name), you in fact lisp out the sense of pleasantness and goodness. You are therefore vilifying in harmless men even the harmless name we bear, which is not inconvenient for the tongue, nor harsh to the ear, nor injurious to a single being, nor rude for our country, being a good Greek word, as many others also are, and pleasant in sound and sense. Surely, surely, names are not things which deserve punishment by the sword, or the cross, or the beasts.

Chapter IV.—The Truth Hated in the Christians; So in Measure Was It, of Old, in Socrates. The Virtues of the Christians.

But the sect, you say, is punished in the name of its founder. Now in the first place it is, no doubt, a fair and usual custom that a sect should be marked out by the name of its founder, since philosophers are called Pythagoreans and Platonists after their masters; in the same way physicians are called after Erasistratus, and grammarians after Aristarchus. If, therefore, a sect has a bad character because its founder was bad, it is punished as the traditional bearer of a bad name. But this would be indulging in a rash assumption. The first step was to find out what the founder was, that his sect might be understood, instead of hindering inquiry into the founder's character from the sect. But in our case, by being necessarily ignorant of the sect, through your ignorance of its founder, or else by not taking a fair survey of the founder, because you make no inquiry into his sect, you fasten merely on the name, just as if you vilified in it both sect and founder, whom you know nothing of whatever. And yet you openly allow your philosophers the right of attaching themselves to any school, and bearing its founder's name as their own; and nobody stirs up any hatred against them, although both in public and in private they bark out their bitterest eloquence against your customs, rites, ceremonies, and manner of life, with so much contempt for the laws, and so little respect for persons, that they even flaunt their licentious words against the emperors themselves with impunity. And yet it is the truth, which is so troublesome to the world, that these philosophers affect, but which Christians possess: they therefore who have it in possession afford the greater displeasure, because he who affects a thing plays with it; he who possesses it maintains it. For example, Socrates was condemned on that side (of his wisdom) in which he came nearest in his search to the truth, by destroying your gods. Although the name of Christian was not at that time in the world, yet truth was always suffering condemnation. Now you will not deny that he was a wise man, to whom your own Pythian (god) had borne witness. Socrates, he said, was the wisest of men. Truth overbore Apollo, and made him pronounce even against himself since he acknowledged that he was no god, when he affirmed that that was the wisest man who was denying the gods. However, on your principle he was the less wise because he denied the gods, although, in truth, he was all the wiser by reason of this denial. It is just in the same way that you are in the habit of saying of us: "Lucius Titius is a good man, only he is a Christian;" while another says; "I wonder that so worthy a man as Caius Seius has become a Christian." According to the blindness of their folly men praise what they know, (and) blame what they are ignorant of; and that which they know, they vitiate by that which they do not know. It occurs to none (to consider) whether a man is not good and wise because he is a Christian, or therefore a Christian because he is wise and good, although it is more usual in human conduct to determine obscurities by what is manifest, than to prejudice what is manifest by what is obscure. Some persons wonder that those whom they had known to be unsteady, worthless, *or* wicked before they bore this name, have been suddenly converted to virtuous courses; and yet they better know how to wonder (at the change) than to attain to it; others are so obstinate in their strife as to do battle with their own best interests, which they have it in their power to secure by intercourse with that hated name. I know more than one husband, formerly anxious about their wives' conduct, and unable to bear even mice to creep into their bed-room without a groan of suspicion, who have, upon discovering the cause of their new assiduity, and their unwonted attention to the duties of home, offered the entire loan of their wives to others, disclaimed all jealousy, (and) preferred to be the husbands of she-wolves than of Christian women: they could commit themselves to a perverse abuse of nature, but they could not permit their wives to be reformed for the better! A father disinherited his son, with whom he had ceased to find fault. A master sent his slave to bridewell, whom he had even found to be indispensable to him. As soon as they discovered them to be Christians, they wished they were criminals again; for our discipline carries its own evidence in itself, nor are we betrayed by anything else than our own goodness, just as bad men also become conspicuous by their own evil. Else how is it that we alone are, contrary to the lessons of nature, branded as very evil because of our good? For what mark do we exhibit except the prime wisdom, which teaches us not to worship the frivolous works of the human hand; the temperance, by which we abstain from other men's goods; the chastity, which we pollute not even with a look; the compassion, which prompts us to help the needy; the truth itself, which makes us give offence; and liberty, for which we have even learned to die? Whoever wishes to understand who the Christians are, must needs employ these marks for their discovery.

Chapter V.—The Inconsistent Life of Any False Christian No More Condemns True Disciples of Christ, Than a Passing Cloud Obscures a Summer Sky.

As to your saying of us that we are a most shameful set, and utterly steeped in luxury, avarice, and depravity, we will not deny that this is true of some. It is, however, a sufficient testimonial for our name, that this cannot be said of all, not even of the greater part of us. It must happen even in the healthiest and purest body, that a mole should grow, or a wart arise on it, or freckles disfigure it. Not even the sky itself is clear with so perfect a serenity as not to be flecked with some filmy cloud. A slight spot on the face, because it is obvious in so conspicuous a part, only serves to show purity of the entire complexion. The goodness of the larger portion is well attested by the slender flaw. But although you prove that some of our people are evil, you do not hereby prove that they are Christians. Search and see whether there is any sect to which (a partial shortcoming) is imputed as a general stain. You are accustomed in conversation yourselves to say, in disparagement of us, "Why is soand-so deceitful, when the Christians are so self-denying? why merciless, when they are so merciful?" You thus bear your testimony to the fact that this is not the character of Christians, when you ask, in the way of a retort, how men who are reputed to be Christians can be of such and such a disposition. There is a good deal of difference between an imputation and a name, between an opinion and the truth. For names were appointed for the express purpose of setting their proper limits between mere designation and actual condition. How many indeed are said to be philosophers, who for all that do not fulfill the law of philosophy? All bear the name in respect of their profession; but they hold the designation without the excellence of the profession, and they disgrace the real thing under the shallow pretence of its name. Men are not straightway of such and such a character, because they are said to be so; but when they are not, it is vain to say so of them: they only deceive people who attach reality to a name, when it is its consistency with fact which decides the condition implied in the name. And yet persons of this doubtful stamp do not assemble with us, neither do they belong to our communion: by their delinquency they become yours once more since we should be unwilling to mix even with them whom your violence and cruelty compelled to recant. Yet we should, of course, be more ready to have included amongst us those who have unwillingly forsaken our discipline than willful apostates. However, you have no right to call them Christians, to whom the Christians themselves deny that name, and who have not learned to deny themselves.

Chapter VI.—The Innocence of the Christians Not Compromised by the Iniquitous Laws Which Were Made Against Them.

Whenever these statements and answers of ours, which truth suggests of its own accord, press and restrain your conscience, which is the witness of its own ignorance, you betake yourselves in hot haste to that poor altar of refuge, the authority of the laws, because these, of course, would never punish the offensive sect, if their deserts had not been fully considered by those who made the laws. Then what is it which has prevented a like consideration on the part of those who put the laws in force, when, in the case of all other crimes which are similarly forbidden and punished by the laws, the penalty is not inflicted until it is sought by regular process? Take, for instance, the case of a murderer or an adulterer. An examination is ordered touching the particulars of the crime, even though it is patent to all what its nature is. Whatever wrong has been done by the Christian ought to be brought to light. No law forbids inquiry to be made; on the contrary, inquiry is made in the interest of the laws. For how are you to keep the law by precautions against that which the law forbids, if you neutralize the carefulness of the precaution by your failing to perceive what it is you have to keep? No law must keep to itself the knowledge of its own righteousness, but (it owes it) to those from whom it claims obedience. The law, however, becomes an object of suspicion when it declines to approve itself. Naturally enough, then, are the laws against the Christians supposed to be just and deserving of respect and observance, just as long as men remain ignorant of their aim and purport; but when this is perceived, their extreme injustice is discovered, and they are deservedly rejected with abhorrence, along with (their instruments of torture)—the swords, the crosses, and the lions. An unjust law secures no respect. In my opinion, however, there is a suspicion among you that some of these laws are unjust, since not a day passes without your modifying their severity and iniquity by fresh deliberations and decisions.

Chapter VII.—The Christians Defamed. A Sarcastic Description of Fame; Its Deception and Atrocious Slanders of the Christians Lengthily Described.

Whence comes it to pass, you will say to us, that such a character could have been attributed to you, as to have justified the lawmakers perhaps by its imputation? Let me ask on my side, what voucher they had then, or you now, for the truth of the imputation? (You answer,) Fame. Well, now, is not this—"Fama malum, quo non aliud velocius ullum?" Now, why *a plague*, if it be always true? It never ceases from lying; nor even at the moment when it reports the truth is it so free from the wish to lie, as not to interweave the false with the true, by processes of addition, diminution, or confusion of various facts. Indeed, such is its condition, that it can only continue to exist while it lies. For it lives only just so long as it fails to prove anything. As soon as it proves itself true, it falls; and, as if its office of reporting news were at an end, it quits its post: thenceforward the thing is held to be a fact, and it passes under that name. No one, then, says, to take an instance, "The report is that this happened at Rome," or, "The rumor goes that he has got a province;" but, "He has got a province," and, "This happened at Rome." Nobody mentions a rumor except at an uncertainty, because nobody can be sure of a rumor, but only of certain knowledge; and none but a fool believes a rumor, because no wise man puts faith in an uncertainty. In however wide a circuit a report has been circulated, it must needs have originated some time or other from one mouth; afterwards it creeps on somehow to ears and tongues which pass it on and so obscures the humble error in which it began, that no one considers whether the mouth which first set it a-going disseminated a falsehood,—a circumstance which often happens either from a temper of rivalry, or a suspicious turn, or even the pleasure of feigning news. It is, however, well that time reveals all things, as your own sayings and proverbs testify; yea, as nature herself attests, which has so ordered it that nothing lies hid, not even that which fame has not reported. See, now, what a witness you have suborned against us: it has not been able up to this time to prove the report it set in motion, although it has had so long a time to recommend it to our acceptance. This name of ours took its rise in the reign of Augustus; under Tiberius it was taught with all clearness and publicity; under Nero it was ruthlessly condemned, and you may weigh its worth and character even from the person of its persecutor. If that prince was a pious man, then the Christians are impious; if he was just, if he was pure, then the Christians are unjust and impure; if he was not a public enemy, we are enemies of our country: what sort of men we are, our persecutor himself shows, since he of course punished what produced hostility to himself. Now, although every other institution which existed under Nero has been destroyed, yet this of ours has firmly remained—righteous, it would seem, as being unlike the author (of its persecution). Two hundred and fifty years, then, have not yet passed since our life began. During the interval there have been so many criminals; so many crosses have obtained immortality; so many infants have been slain; so many loaves steeped in blood; so many extinctions of candles; so many dissolute marriages. And up to the present time it is mere report which fights against the Christians. No doubt it has a strong support in the wickedness of the human mind, and utters its falsehoods with more success among cruel and savage men. For the more inclined you are to maliciousness, the more ready are you to believe evil; in short, men more easily believe the evil that is false, than the good which is true. Now, if injustice has left any place within you for the exercise of prudence in investigating the truth of reports, justice of course demanded that you should examine by whom the report could have been spread among the multitude, and thus circulated through the world. For it could not have been by the Christians themselves, I suppose, since by the very constitution and law of all mysteries the obligation of silence is imposed. How much more would this be the case in such (mysteries as are ascribed to us), which, if divulged, could not fail to bring down instant punishment from the prompt resentment of men! Since, therefore, the Christians are not their own betrayers, it follows that it must be strangers. Now I ask, how could strangers obtain knowledge of us, when even true and lawful mysteries exclude every stranger from witnessing them, unless illicit ones are less exclusive? Well, then, it is more in keeping with the character of strangers both to be ignorant (of the true state of a case), and to invent (a false account). Our domestic servants (perhaps) listened, and peeped through crevices and holes, and stealthily got information of our ways. What, then, shall we say when our servants betray them to you? It is better, (to be sure,) for us all not to be betrayed by any; but still, if our practices be so atrocious, how much more proper is it when a righteous indignation bursts asunder even all ties of domestic fidelity? How was it possible for it to endure what horrified the mind and affrighted the eye? This is also a wonderful thing, both that he who was so overcome with impatient excitement as to turn informer, did not likewise desire to prove (what he reported), and that he who heard the informer's story did not care to see for himself, since no doubt the reward is equal both for the informer who proves what he reports, and for the hearer who convinces himself of the credibility of what he hears. But then you say that (this is precisely what has taken place): first came the rumor, then the exhibition of the proof; first the hearsay, then the inspection; and after this, fame received its commission. Now this, I must say, surpasses all admiration, that that was once for all detected and divulged which is being forever repeated, unless, forsooth, we have by this time ceased from the reiteration of such things(as are alleged of us). But we are called still by the same (offensive) name, and we are supposed to be still engaged in the same practices, and we multiply from day to day; the more we are, to the more become we objects of hatred. Hatred increases as the material for it increases. Now, seeing that the multitude of offenders is ever advancing, how is it that the crowd of informers does not keep equal pace therewith? To the best of my belief, even our manner of life has become better known; you know the very days of our assemblies; therefore we are both besieged, and attacked, and kept prisoners actually in our secret congregations. Yet who ever came upon a half-consumed corpse (amongst us)? Who has detected the traces of a bite in our blood-steeped loaf? Who has discovered, by a sudden light invading our darkness, any marks of impurity, I will not say of incest, (in our feasts)? If we save ourselves by a bribe from being dragged out before the public gaze with such a character, how is it that we are still oppressed? We have it indeed in our own power not to be thus apprehended at all; for who either sells or buys information about a crime, if the crime itself has no existence? But why need I disparagingly refer to strange spies and informers, when you allege against us such charges as we certainly do not ourselves divulge with very much noise—either as soon as you hear of them, if we previously show them to you, or after you have yourselves discovered them, if they are for the time concealed from you? For no doubt, when any desire initiation in the mysteries, their custom is first to go to the master or father of the sacred rites. Then he will say (to the applicant), You must bring an infant, as a guarantee for our rites, to be sacrificed, as well as some bread to be broken and dipped in his blood; you also want candles, and dogs tied together to upset them, and bits of meat to rouse the dogs. Moreover, a mother too, or a sister, is necessary for you. What, however, is to be said if you have neither? I suppose in that case you could not be a genuine Christian. Now, do let me ask you, Will such things, when reported by strangers, bear to be spread about (as charges against us)? It is impossible for such persons to understand proceedings in which they take no part. The first step of the process is perpetrated with artifice; our feasts and our marriages are invented and detailed by ignorant persons, who had never before heard about Christian mysteries. And though they afterwards cannot help acquiring some knowledge of them, it is even then as having to be administered by others whom they bring on the scene. Besides, how absurd is it that the profane know mysteries which the priest knows not! They keep them all to themselves, then, and take them for granted; and so these tragedies, (worse than those) of Thyestes or OEdipus, do not at all come forth to light, nor find their way to the public. Even more voracious bites take nothing away from the credit of such as are initiated, whether servants or masters. If, however, none of these allegations can be proved to be true, how incalculable must be esteemed the grandeur (of that religion) which is manifestly not overbalanced even by the burden of these vast atrocities! O ye heathen; who have and deserve our pity, behold, we set before you the promise which our sacred system offers. It guarantees eternal life to such as follow and observe it; on the other hand, it threatens with the eternal punishment of an unending fire those who are profane and hostile; while to both classes alike is preached a resurrection from the dead. We are not now concerned about the doctrine of these (verities), which are discussed in their proper place. Meanwhile, however, believe them, even as we do ourselves, for I want to know whether you are ready to reach them, as we do, through such crimes. Come, whosoever you are, plunge your sword into an infant; or if that is another's office, then simply gaze at the breathing creature dying before it has lived; at any rate, catch its fresh blood in which to steep your bread; then feed yourself without stint; and whilst this is going on, recline. Carefully distinguish the places where your mother or your sister may have made their bed; mark them well, in order that, when the shades of night have fallen upon them, putting of course to the test the care of every one of you, you may not make the awkward mistake of alighting on somebody else: you would have to make an atonement, if you failed of the incest. When you have effected all this, eternal life will be in store for you. I want you to tell me whether you think eternal life worth such a price. No, indeed, you do not believe it: even if you did believe it, I maintain that you would be unwilling to give (the fee); or if willing, would be unable. But why should others be able if you are unable? Why should you be able if others are unable? What would you wish impunity (and) eternity to stand you in? Do you suppose that these (blessings) can be bought by us at any price? Have Christians teeth of a different sort from others? Have they more ample jaws? Are they of different nerve for incestuous lust? I trow not. It is enough for us to differ from you in condition by truth alone.

Chapter VIII.—The Calumny Against the Christians Illustrated in the Discovery of Psammetichus. Refutation of the Story.

We are indeed said to be the "third race" of men. What, a dog-faced race? Or broadly shadow-footed? Or some subterranean Antipodes? If you attach any meaning to these names, pray tell us what are the first and the second race, that so we may know something of this "third." Psammetichus thought that he had hit upon the ingenious discovery of the primeval man. He is said to have removed certain new-born infants from all human intercourse, and to have entrusted them to a nurse, whom he had previously deprived of her tongue, in order that, being completely exiled from all sound of the human voice, they might form their speech without hearing it; and thus, deriving it from themselves alone, might indicate what that first nation was whose speech was dictated by nature. Their first utterance was Bekkos, a word which means *"bread"* in the language of Phrygia: the Phrygians, therefore, are supposed to be the first of the human race. But it will not be out of place if we make one observation, with a view to show how your faith abandons itself more to vanities than to verities. Can it be, then, at all credible that the nurse retained her life, after the loss of so important a member, the very organ of the breath of life,—cut out, too, from the very root, with her throat mutilated, which cannot be wounded even on the outside without danger, and the putrid gore flowing back to the chest, and deprived for so long a time of her food? Come, even suppose that by the remedies of a Philomela she retained her life, in the way supposed by wisest persons, who account for the dumbness not by cutting out the tongue, but from the blush of shame; if on such a supposition she lived, she would still be able to blurt out some dull sound. And a shrill inarticulate noise from opening the mouth only, without any modulation of the lips, might be forced from the mere throat, though there were no tongue to help. This, it is probable, the infants readily imitated, and the more so because it was the only sound; only they did it a little more neatly, as they had tongues; and then they attached to it a definite signification. Granted, then, that the Phrygians were the earliest race, it does not follow that the Christians are the third. For how many other nations come regularly after the Phrygians? Take care, however, lest those whom you call the third race should obtain the first rank, since there is no nation indeed which is not Christian. Whatever nation, therefore, was the first, is nevertheless Christian now. It is ridiculous folly which makes you say we are the latest race, and then specifically call us the third. But it is in respect of our religion, not of our nation, that we are supposed to be the third; the series being the Romans, the Jews, and the Christians after them. Where, then, are the Greeks? or if they are reckoned amongst the Romans in regard to their superstition (since it was from Greece that Rome borrowed even her gods), where at least are the Egyptians, since these have, so far as I know, a mysterious religion peculiar to themselves? Now, if they who belong to the third race are so monstrous, what must they be supposed to be who preceded them in the first and the second place?

Chapter IX.—The Christians are Not the Cause of Public Calamities: There Were Such Troubles Before Christianity.

But why should I be astonished at your vain imputations? Under the same natural form, malice and folly have always been associated in one body and growth, and have ever opposed us under the one instigator of error. Indeed, I feel no astonishment; and therefore, as it is necessary for my subject, I will enumerate some instances, that you may feel the astonishment by the enumeration of the folly into which you fall, when you insist on our being the causes of every public calamity or injury. If the Tiber has overflowed its banks, if the Nile has remained in its bed, if the sky has been still, or the earth been in commotion, if death has made its devastations, or famine its afflictions, your cry immediately is, "This is the fault of the Christians!" As if they who fear the true God could have to fear a light thing, or at least anything else (than an earthquake or famine, or such visitations). I suppose it is as despisers of your gods that we call down on us these strokes of theirs. As we have remarked already, three hundred years have not yet passed in our existence; but what vast scourges before that time fell on all the world, on its various cities and provinces! what terrible wars, both foreign and domestic! what pestilences, famines, conflagrations, yawnings, and quakings of the earth has history recorded! Where were the Christians, then, when the Roman state furnished so many chronicles of its disasters? Where were the Christians when the islands Hiera, Anaphe, and Delos, and Rhodes, and Cea were desolated with multitudes of men? or, again, when the land mentioned by Plato as larger than Asia or Africa was sunk in the Atlantic Sea? or when fire from heaven overwhelmed Volsinii, and flames from their own mountain consumed Pompeii? when the sea of Corinth was engulfed by an earthquake? when the whole world was destroyed by the deluge? Where *then* were (I will not say the Christians, who despise your gods, but) your gods themselves, who are proved to be of later origin than that great ruin by the very places and cities in which they were born, sojourned, and were buried, and even those which they founded? For else they would not have remained to the present day, unless they had been more recent than that catastrophe. If you do not care to peruse and reflect upon these testimonies of history, the record of which affects you differently from us, in order especially that you may not have to tax your gods with extreme injustice, since they injure even their worshippers on account of their despisers, do you not then prove yourselves to be also in the wrong, when you hold them to be gods, who make no distinction between the deserts of yourselves and profane persons? If, however, as it is now and then very vainly said, you incur the chastisement of your gods because you are too slack in our extirpation, you then have settled the question of their weakness and insignificance; for they would not be angry with you for loitering over our punishment, if they could do anything themselves,—although you admit the same thing indeed in another way, whenever by inflicting punishment on us you seem to be avenging them. If one interest is maintained by another party, that which defends is the greater of the two. What a shame, then, must it be for gods to be defended by a human being!

Chapter X.—The Christians are Not the Only Contemners of the Gods. Contempt of Them Often Displayed by Heathen Official Persons. Homer Made the Gods Contemptible.

Pour out now all your venom; fling against this name of ours all your shafts of calumny: I shall stay no longer to refute them; but they shall by and by be blunted, when we come to explain our entire discipline. I shall content myself now indeed with plucking these shafts out of our own body, and hurling them back on yourselves. The same wounds which you have inflicted on us by your charges I shall show to be imprinted on yourselves, that you may fall by your own swords and javelins. Now, first, when you direct against us the general charge of divorcing ourselves from the institutions of our forefathers, consider again and again whether you are not yourselves open to that accusation in common with us. For when I look through your life and customs, lo, what do I discover but the old order of things corrupted, nay, destroyed by you? Of the laws I have already said, that you are daily supplanting them with novel decrees and statutes. As to everything else in your manner of life, how great are the changes you have made from your ancestors—in your style, your dress, your equipage, your very food, and even in your speech; for the old-fashioned you banish, as if it were offensive to you! Everywhere, in your public pursuits and private duties, antiquity is repealed; all the authority of your forefathers your own authority has superseded. To be sure, you are forever praising old customs; but this is only to your greater discredit, for you nevertheless persistently reject them. How great must your perverseness have been, to have bestowed approbation on your ancestors' institutions, which were too inefficient to be lasting, all the while that you were rejecting the very objects of your approbation! But even that very heir-loom of your forefathers, which you seem to guard and defend with greatest fidelity, in which you actually find your strongest grounds for impeaching us as violators of the law, and from which your hatred of the Christian name derives all its life—I mean the worship of the gods—I shall prove to be undergoing ruin and contempt from yourselves no less than (from us),—unless it be that there is no reason for our being regarded as despisers of the gods like yourselves, on the ground that nobody despises what he knows has absolutely no existence. What certainly exists can be despised. That which *is* nothing, suffers nothing. From those, therefore, to whom it is an existing thing, must necessarily proceed the suffering which affects it. All the heavier, then, is the accusation which burdens you who believe that there are gods and (at the same time) despise them, who worship and also reject them, who honor and also assail them. One may also gather the same conclusion from this consideration, above all: since you worship various gods, someone and some another, you of course despise those which you do not worship. A preference for the one is not possible without slighting the other, and no choice can be made without a rejection. He who selects someo*ne* out of many, has already slighted the other which he does not select. But it is impossible that so many and so great gods can be worshipped by all. Then you must have exercised your contempt (in this matter) even at the beginning, since indeed you were not then afraid of so ordering things, that all the gods could not become objects of worship to all. For those very wise and prudent ancestors of yours, whose institutions you know not how to repeal, especially in respect of your gods, are themselves found to have been impious. I am much mistaken, if they did not sometimes decree that no general should dedicate a temple, which he may have vowed in battle, before the senate gave its sanction; as in the case of Marcus Æmilius, who had made a vow to the god **Alburnus**. Now is it not confessedly the greatest impiety, nay, the greatest insult, to place the honor of the Deity at the will and pleasure of human judgment, so that there cannot be a god except the senate permit him? Many times have the censors destroyed (a god) without consulting the people. Father Bacchus, with all his ritual, was certainly by the consuls, on the senate's authority, cast not only out of the city, but out of all Italy; whilst Varro informs us that Serapis also, and Isis, and Arpocrates, and Anubis, were excluded from the Capitol, and that their altars which the senate had thrown down were only restored by the popular violence. The Consul Gabinius, however, on the first day of the ensuing January, although he gave a tardy consent to some sacrifices, in deference to the crowd which assembled, because he had failed to decide about Serapis and Isis, yet held the judgment of the senate to be more potent than the clamor of the multitude, and forbade the altars to be built. Here, then, you have amongst your own forefathers, if not the name, at all events the procedure, of the Christians, which despises the gods. If, however, you were even innocent of the charge of treason against them in the honor you pay them, I still find that you have made a consistent advance in superstition as well as impiety. For how much more irreligious are you found to be! There are your household gods, the Lares and the Penates, which you possess by a family consecration: you even tread them profanely under foot, you and your domestics, by hawking and pawning them for your wants or your whims. Such insolent sacrilege might be excusable, if it were not practiced against your humbler deities; as it is, the case is only the more insolent. There is, however, some consolation for your private household gods under these affronts, that you treat your public deities with still greater indignity and insolence. First of all, you advertise them for auction, submit them to public sale, knock them down to the highest bidder, when you every five years bring them to the hammer among your revenues. For this purpose you frequent the temple of Serapis or the Capitol, hold your sales there, conclude your contracts, as if they were markets, with the well-known voice of the crier, (and) the self-same levy of the quæstor. Now lands become cheaper when burdened with tribute, and men by the capitation tax diminish in value (these are the well-known marks of slavery). But the gods, the more tribute they pay, become more holy; or rather, the more holy they are, the more tribute do they pay. Their majesty is converted into an article of traffic; men drive a business with their religion; the sanctity of the gods is beggared with sales and contracts. You make merchandise of the ground of your temples, of the approach to your altars, of your offerings, of your sacrifices. You sell the whole divinity (of your gods). You will not permit their gratuitous worship. The auctioneers necessitate more repairs than the priests.

It was not enough that you had insolently made a profit of your gods, if we would test the amount of your contempt; and you are not content to have withheld honor from them, you must also depreciate the little you do render to them by some indignity or other. What, indeed, do you do by way of honoring your gods, which you do not equally offer to your dead? You build temples for the gods, you erect temples also to the dead; you build altars for the gods, you build them also for the dead; you inscribe the same superscription over both; you sketch out the same lineaments for their statues—as best suits their genius, or profession, or age; you make an old man of Saturn, a beardless youth of Apollo; you form a virgin from Diana; in Mars you consecrate a soldier, a blacksmith in Vulcan. No wonder, therefore, if you slay the same victims and burn the same odors for your dead as you do for your gods. What excuse can be found for that insolence which classes the dead of whatever sort as equal with the gods? Even to your princes there are assigned the services of priests and sacred ceremonies, and chariots, and cars, and the honors of the *solisternia* and the *lectisternia*, holidays and games. Rightly enough, since heaven is open to them; still it is none the less contumelious to the gods: in the first place, because it could not possibly be decent that other beings should be numbered with them, even if it has been given to them to become divine after their birth; in the second place, because the witness who beheld the man caught up into heaven would not forswear himself so freely and palpably before the people, if it were not for the contempt felt about the objects sworn to both by himself and those who allow the perjury. For these feel of themselves, that what is sworn to is nothing; and more than that, they go so far as to fee the witness, because he had the courage to publicly despise the avengers of perjury. Now, as to that, who among you is pure of the charge of perjury? By this time, indeed, there is an end to all danger in swearing by the gods, since the oath by Cæsar carries with it more influential scruples, which very circumstance indeed tends to the degradation of your gods; for those who perjure themselves when swearing by Cæsar are more readily punished than those who violate an oath to a Jupiter. But, of the two kindred feelings of contempt and derision, contempt is the more honorable, having a certain glory in its arrogance; for it sometimes proceeds from confidence, or the security of consciousness, or a natural loftiness of mind. Derision, however, is a more wanton feeling, and so far it points more directly to a carping insolence. Now only consider what great deriders of your gods you show yourselves to be! I say nothing of your indulgence of this feeling during your sacrificial acts, how you offer for your victims the poorest and most emaciated creatures; or else of the sound and healthy animals only the portions which are useless for food, such as the heads and hoofs, or the plucked feathers and hair, and whatever at home you would have thrown away. I pass over whatever may seem to the taste of the vulgar and profane to have constituted the religion of your forefathers; but then the most learned and serious classes (for seriousness and wisdom to some extent profess to be derived from learning) are always, in fact, the most irreverent towards your gods; and if their learning ever halts, it is only to make up for the remissness by a more shameful invention of follies and falsehoods about their gods. I will begin with that enthusiastic fondness which you show for him from whom every depraved writer gets his dreams, to whom you ascribe as much honor as you derogate from your gods, by magnifying him who has made such sport of them. I mean Homer by this description. He it is, in my opinion, who has treated the majesty of the Divine Being on the low level of human condition, imbuing the gods with the falls and the passions of men; who has pitted them against each other with varying success, like pairs of gladiators: he wounds Venus with an arrow from a human hand; he keeps Mars a prisoner in chains for thirteen months, with the prospect of perishing; he parades Jupiter as suffering a like indignity from a crowd of celestial (rebels;) or he draws from him tears for Sarpedon; or he represents him wantoning with Juno in the most disgraceful way, advocating his incestuous passion for her by a description and enumeration of his various amours. Since then, which of the poets has not, on the authority of their great prince, calumniated the gods, by either betraying truth or feigning falsehood? Have the dramatists also, whether in tragedy or comedy, refrained from making the gods the authors of the calamities and retributions (of their plays)? I say nothing of your philosophers, whom a certain inspiration of truth itself elevates against the gods, and secures from all fear in their proud severity and stern discipline. Take, for example, Socrates. In contempt of your gods, he swears by an oak, and a dog, and a goat. Now, although he was condemned to die for this very reason, the Athenians afterwards repented of that condemnation, and even put to death his accusers. By this conduct of theirs the testimony of Socrates is replaced at its full value, and I am enabled to meet you with this retort, that in his case you have approbation bestowed on that which is now-a-days reprobated in us. But besides this instance there is Diogenes, who, I know not to what extent, made sport of Hercules; whilst Varro, that Diogenes of the Roman cut, introduces to our view some three hundred Joves, or, as they ought to be called, Jupiters, (and all) without heads. Your other wanton wits likewise minister to your pleasures by disgracing the gods. Examine carefully the sacrilegious beauties of your Lentuli and Hostii; now, is it the players or your gods who become the objects of your mirth in their tricks and jokes? Then, again, with what pleasure do you take up the literature of the stage, which describes all the foul conduct of the gods! Their majesty is defiled in your presence in some unchaste body. The mask of some deity, at your will, covers some infamous paltry head. The Sun mourns for the death of his son by a lightning-flash amid your rude rejoicing. Cybele sighs for a shepherd who disdains her, without raising a blush on your cheek; and you quietly endure songs which celebrate the gallantries of Jove. You are, of course, possessed of a more religious spirit in the show of your gladiators, when your gods dance, with equal zest, over the spilling of human blood, (and) over those filthy penalties which are at once their proof and plot for executing your criminals, or else (when) your criminals are punished personating the gods themselves. We have often witnessed in a mutilated criminal your god of Pessinum, Attis; a wretch burnt alive has personated Hercules. We have laughed at the sport of your mid-day game of the gods, when Father Pluto, Jove's own brother, drags away, hammer in hand, the remains of the gladiators; when Mercury, with his winged cap and heated wand, tests with his cautery whether the bodies were really lifeless, or only feigning death. Who now can investigate every particular of this sort although so destructive of the honor of the Divine Being, and so humiliating to His majesty? They all, indeed, have their origin in a contempt (of the gods), on the part both of those who practice these personations, as well as of those who are susceptible of being so represented. I hardly know, therefore, whether your gods have more reason to complain of yourselves or of us. After despising them on the one hand, you flatter them on the other; if you fail in any duty towards them, you appease them with a fee; in short, you allow yourselves to act towards them in any way you please. We, however, live in a consistent and entire aversion to them.

Chapter XI.—The Absurd Cavil of the Ass's Head Disposed of.

In this matter we are (said to be) guilty not merely of forsaking the religion of the community, but of introducing a monstrous superstition; for some among you have dreamed that our god is an ass's head,—an absurdity which Cornelius Tacitus first suggested. In the fourth book of his *histories*, where he is treating of the Jewish war, he begins his description with the origin of that nation, and gives his own views respecting both the origin and the name of their religion. He relates that the Jews, in their migration in the desert, when suffering for want of water, escaped by following for guides some wild asses, which they supposed to be going in quest of water after pasture, and that on this account the image of one of these animals was worshipped by the Jews. From this, I suppose, it was presumed that we, too, from our close connection with the Jewish religion, have ours consecrated under the same emblematic form. The same Cornelius Tacitus, however,—who, to say the truth, is most loquacious in falsehood—forgetting his later statement, relates how Pompey the Great, after conquering the Jews and capturing Jerusalem, entered the temple, but found nothing in the shape of an image, though he examined the place carefully. Where, then, should their God have been found? Nowhere else, of course, than in so memorable a temple which was carefully shut to all but the priests, and into which there could be no fear of a stranger entering. But what apology must I here offer for what I am going to say, when I have no other object at the moment than to make a passing remark or two in a general way which shall be equally applicable to yourselves? Suppose that our God, then, be an asinine person, will you at all events deny that you possess the same characteristics with ourselves in that matter? (Not their heads only, but) entire asses, are, to be sure, objects of adoration to you, along with their tutelar Epona; and all herds, and cattle, and beasts you consecrate, and their stables into the bargain! This, perhaps, is your grievance against us, that, when surrounded by cattle-worshippers of every kind we are simply devoted to asses!

Chapter XII.—The Charge of Worshipping a Cross. The Heathens Themselves Made Much of Crosses in Sacred Things; Nay, Their Very Idols Were Formed on a Crucial Frame.

As for him who affirms that we are "the priesthood of a cross," we shall claim him as our co-religionist. A cross is, in its material, a sign of wood; amongst yourselves also the object of worship is a wooden figure. Only, whilst with you the figure is a human one, with us the wood is its own figure. Never mind for the present what is the shape, provided the material is the same: the form, too, is of no importance, if so be it be the actual body of a god. If, however, there arises a question of difference on this point what, (let me ask,) is the difference between the Athenian Pallas, or the Pharian Ceres, and wood formed into a cross, when each is represented by a rough stock, without form, and by the merest rudiment of a statue of unformed wood? Every piece of timber which is fixed in the ground in an erect position is a part of a cross, and indeed the greater portion of its mass. But an entire cross is attributed to us, with its transverse beam, of course, and its projecting seat. Now you have the less to excuse you, for you dedicate to religion only a mutilated imperfect piece of wood, while others consecrate to the sacred purpose a complete structure. The truth, however, after all is, that your religion is *all cross*, as I shall show. You are indeed unaware that your gods in their origin have proceeded from this hated cross. Now, every image, whether carved out of wood or stone, or molten in metal, or produced out of any other richer material, must needs have had plastic hands engaged in its formation. Well, then, this modeler, before he did anything else, hit upon the form of a wooden cross, because even our own body assumes as its natural position the latent and concealed outline of a cross.

Since the head rises upwards, and the back takes a straight direction, and the shoulders project laterally, if you simply place a man with his arms and hands outstretched, you will make the general outline of a cross. Starting, then, from this rudimental form and prop, as it were, he applies a covering of clay, and so gradually completes the limbs, and forms the body, and covers the cross within with the shape which he meant to impress upon the clay; then from this design, with the help of compasses and leaden moulds, he has got all ready for his image which is to be brought out into marble, or clay, or whatever the material be of which he has determined to make his god. (This, then, is the process:) after the cross-shaped frame, the clay; after the clay, the god. In a well-understood routine, the cross passes into a god through the clayey medium. The cross then you consecrate, and from it the consecrated (deity) begins to derive his origin. By way of example, let us take the case of a tree which grows up into a system of branches and foliage, and is a reproduction of its own kind, whether it springs from the kernel of an olive, or the stone of a peach, or a grain of pepper which has been duly tempered underground. Now, if you transplant it, or take a cutting off its branches for another plant, to what will you attribute what is produced by the propagation? Will it not be to the grain, or the stone, or the kernel? Because, as the third stage is attributable to the second, and the second in like manner to the first, so the third will have to be referred to the first, through the second as the mean. We need not stay any longer in the discussion of this point, since by a natural law every kind of produce throughout nature refers back its growth to its original source; and just as the product is comprised in its primal cause, so does that cause agree in character with the thing produced. Since, then, in the production of your gods, you worship the cross which originates them, here will be the original kernel and grain, from which are propagated the wooden materials of your idolatrous images. Examples are not far to seek. Your victories you celebrate with religious ceremony as deities; and they are the more august in proportion to the joy they bring you. The frames on which you hang up your trophies must be crosses: these are, as it were, the very core of your pageants. Thus, in your victories, the religion of your camp makes even crosses objects of worship; your standards it adores, your standards are the sanction of its oaths; your standards it prefers before Jupiter himself. But all that parade of images, and that display of pure gold, are (as so many) necklaces of the crosses. In like manner also, in the banners and ensigns, which your soldiers guard with no less sacred care, you have the streamers (and) vestments of your crosses. You are ashamed, I suppose, to worship unadorned and simple crosses.

Chapter XIII.—The Charge of Worshipping the Sun Met by a Retort.

Others, with greater regard to good manners, it must be confessed, suppose that the sun is the god of the Christians, because it is a well-known fact that we pray towards the east, or because we make Sunday a day of festivity. What then? Do you do less than this? Do not many among you, with an affectation of sometimes worshipping the heavenly bodies likewise, move your lips in the direction of the sunrise? It is you, at all events, who have even admitted the sun into the calendar of the week; and you have selected its day, in preference to the preceding day as the most suitable in the week for either an entire abstinence from the bath, or for its postponement until the evening, or for taking rest and for banqueting. By resorting to these customs, you deliberately deviate from your own religious rites to those of strangers. For the Jewish feasts on the Sabbath and "the Purification," and Jewish also are the ceremonies of the lamps, and the fasts of unleavened bread, and the "littoral prayers," all which institutions and practices are of course foreign from your gods. Wherefore, that I may return from this digression, you who reproach us with the sun and Sunday should consider your proximity to us. We are not far off from your Saturn and your days of rest.

Chapter XIV.—The Vile Calumny About Onocoetes Retorted on the Heathen by Tertullian.

Report has introduced a new calumny respecting our God. Not so long ago, a most abandoned wretch in that city of yours, a man who had deserted indeed his own religion—a Jew, in fact, who had only lost his skin, flayed of course by wild beasts, against which he enters the lists for hire day after day with a sound body, and so in a condition to lose his skin—carried about in public a caricature of us with this label: *Onocoetes*. This (figure) had ass's ears, and was dressed in a *toga* with a book, having a hoof on one of his feet. And the crowd believed this infamous Jew. For what other set of men is the seed-plot of all the calumny against us? Throughout the city, therefore, Onocoetes is all the talk. As, however, it is less than "a nine days' wonder," and so destitute of all authority from time, and weak enough from the character of its author, I shall gratify myself by using it simply in the way of a retort. Let us then see whether you are not here also found in our company. Now it matters not what their form may be, when our concern is about deformed images. You have amongst you gods with a dog's head, and a lion's head, with the horns of a cow, and a ram, and a goat, goat-shaped or serpent-shaped, and winged in foot, head, and back. Why therefore brand our one God so conspicuously? Many an *Onocoetes* is found amongst yourselves.

Chapter XV.—The Charge of Infanticide Retorted on the Heathen.

Since we are on a par in respect of the gods, it follows that there is no difference between us on the point of sacrifice, or even of worship, if I may be allowed to make good our comparison from another sort of evidence. We begin our religious service, or initiate our mysteries, with slaying an infant. As for you, since your own transactions in human blood and infanticide have faded from your memory, you shall be duly reminded of them in the proper place; we now postpone most of the instances, that we may not seem to be everywhere handling the selfsame topics. Meanwhile, as I have said, the comparison between us does not fail in another point of view. For if we are infanticides in one sense, you also can hardly be deemed such in any other sense; because, although you are forbidden by the laws to slay new-born infants, it so happens that no laws are evaded with more impunity or greater safety, with the deliberate knowledge of the public, and the suffrages of this entire age. Yet there is no great difference between us, only you do not kill your infants in the way of a sacred rite, nor (as a service) to God. But then you make away with them in a more cruel manner, because you expose them to the cold and hunger, and to wild beasts, or else you get rid of them by the slower death of drowning. If, however, there does occur any dissimilarity between us in this matter, you must not overlook the fact that it is your own dear children whose life you quench; and this will supplement, nay abundantly aggravate, on your side of the question, whatever is defective in us on other grounds. Well, but we are said to sup off our impious sacrifice! Whilst we postpone to a more suitable place whatever resemblance even to this practice is discoverable amongst yourselves, we are not far removed from you in voracity. If in the one case there is unchastity, and in ours cruelty, we are still on the same footing (if I may so far admit our guilt) in nature, where cruelty is always found in concord with unchastity. But, after all, what do you less than we; or rather, what do you not do in excess of us? I wonder whether it be a small matter to you to pant for human entrails, because you devour full-grown men alive? Is it, forsooth, only a trifle to lick up human blood, when you draw out the blood which was destined to live? Is it a light thing in your view to feed on an infant, when you consume one wholly before it is come to the birth?

Chapter XVI.—Other Charges Repelled by the Same Method. The Story of the Noble Roman Youth and His Parents.

I am now come to the hour for extinguishing the lamps, and for using the dogs, and practicing the deeds of darkness. And on this point I am afraid I must succumb to you; for what similar accusation shall I have to bring against you? But you should at once commend the cleverness with which we make our incest look modest, in that we have devised a spurious night, to avoid polluting the real light and darkness, and have even thought it right to dispense with earthly lights, and to play tricks also with our conscience. For whatever we do ourselves, we suspect in others when we choose (to be suspicious). As for your incestuous deeds, on the contrary, men enjoy them at full liberty, in the face of day, or in the natural night, or before high Heaven; and in proportion to their successful issue is your own ignorance of the result, since you publicly indulge in your incestuous intercourse in the full cognizance of broad day-light. (No ignorance, however, conceals our conduct from our eyes,) for in the very darkness we are able to recognize our own misdeeds. The Persians, you know very well, according to Ctesias, live quite promiscuously with their mothers, in full knowledge of the fact, and without any horror; whilst of the Macedonians it is well known that they constantly do the same thing, and with perfect approbation: for once, when the blinded OEdipus came upon their stage, they greeted him with laughter and derisive cheers. The actor, taking off his mask in great alarm, said, "Gentlemen, have I displeased you?" "Certainly not," replied the Macedonians, "you have played your part well enough; but either the author was very silly, if he invented (this mutilation as an atonement for the incest), or else OEdipus was a great fool for his pains if he really so punished himself;" and then they shouted out one to the other, "Ἤλσυνε εἰς τὴν μητέρα.

But how insignificant, (say you,) is the stain which one or two nations can make on the whole world! As for us, we of course have infected the very sun, polluted the entire ocean! Quote, then, one nation which is free from the passions which allure the whole race of men to incest! If there is a single nation which knows nothing of concubinage through the necessity of age and sex—to say nothing of lust and licentiousness—that nation will be a stranger to incest. If any nature can be found so peculiarly removed from the human state as to be liable neither to ignorance, nor error, nor misfortune, that alone may be adduced with any consistency as an answer to the Christians. Reflect, therefore, on the licentiousness which floats about amongst men's passions as if they were the winds, and consider whether there be any communities which the full and strong tides of passion fail to waft to the commission of this great sin. In the first place, when you expose your infants to the mercy of others, or leave them for adoption to better parents than yourselves, do you forget what an opportunity for incest is furnished, how wide a scope is opened for its accidental commission? Undoubtedly, such of you as are more serious from a principle of self-restraint and careful reflection, abstain from lusts which could produce results of such a kind, in whatever place you may happen to be, at home or abroad, so that no indiscriminate diffusion of seed, or licentious reception thereof, will produce children to you unawares, such as their very parents, or else other children, might encounter in inadvertent incest, for no restraint from age is regarded in (the importunities of) lust. All acts of adultery, all cases of fornication, all the licentiousness of public brothels, whether committed at home or perpetrated out of doors, serve to produce confusions of blood and complications of natural relationship, and thence to conduce to incest; from which consummation your players and buffoons draw the materials of their exhibitions. It was from such a source, too, that so flagrant a tragedy recently burst upon the public as that which the prefect Fuscianus had judicially to decide. A boy of noble birth, who, by the unintentional neglect of his attendants, had strolled too far from home, was decoyed by some passers-by, and carried off. The paltry Greek who had the care of him, or somebody else, in true Greek fashion, had gone into the house and captured him. Having been taken away into Asia, he is brought, when arrived at full age, back to Rome, and exposed for sale. His own father buys him unawares, and treats him as a Greek. Afterwards, as was his wont, the youth is sent by his master into the fields, chained as a slave. Thither the tutor and the nurse had already been banished for punishment. The whole case is represented to them; they relate each other's misfortunes: they, on the one hand, how they had lost their ward when he was a boy; he, on the other hand, that he had been lost from his boyhood. But they agreed in the main, that he was a native of Rome of a noble family; perhaps he further gave sure proofs of his identity. Accordingly, as God willed it for the purpose of fastening a stain upon that age, a presentiment about the time excites him, the periods exactly suit his age, even his eyes help to recall his features, some peculiar marks on his body are enumerated. His master and mistress, who are now no other than his own father and mother, anxiously urge a protracted inquiry. The slave-dealer is examined, the unhappy truth is all discovered. When their wickedness becomes manifest, the parents find a remedy for their despair by hanging themselves; to their son, who survives the miserable calamity, their property is awarded by the prefect, not as an inheritance, but as the wages of infamy and incest. That one case was a sufficient example for public exposure of the sins of this sort which are secretly perpetrated among you. Nothing happens among men in solitary isolation. But, as it seems to me, it is only in a solitary case that such a charge can be drawn out against us, even in the mysteries of our religion. You ply us evermore with this charge; yet there are like delinquencies to be traced amongst you, even in your ordinary course of life.

Chapter XVII.—The Christian Refusal to Swear by the Genius of Cæsar. Flippancy and Irreverence Retorted on the Heathen.

As to your charges of obstinacy and presumption, whatever you allege against us, even in these respects, there are not wanting points in which you will bear a comparison with us. Our first step in this contumacious conduct concerns that which is ranked by you immediately after the worship due to God, that is, the worship due to the majesty of the Cæsars, in respect of which we are charged with being irreligious towards them, since we neither propitiate their images nor swear by their genius. We are called enemies of the people. Well, be it so; yet at the same time (it must not be forgotten, that) the emperors find enemies amongst you heathen, and are constantly getting surnames to signalize their triumphs—one becoming *Parthicus*, and another *Medicus* and *Germanicus*. On this head the Roman people must see to it who they are amongst whom there still remain nations which are unsubdued and foreign to their rule. But, at all events, you are of us, and yet you conspire against us. (In reply, we need only state) a well-known fact, that we acknowledge the fealty of Romans to the emperors. No conspiracy has ever broken out from our body: no Cæsar's blood has ever fixed a stain upon us, in the senate or even in the palace; no assumption of the purple has ever in any of the provinces been affected by us. The Syrias still exhale the odors of their corpses; still do the Gauls fail to wash away (their blood) in the waters of their Rhone. Your allegations of our insanity I omit, because they do not compromise the Roman name. But I will grapple with the charge of sacrilegious vanity, and remind you of the irreverence of your own lower classes, and the scandalous lampoons of which the statues are so cognizant, and the sneers which are sometimes uttered at the public games, and the curses with which the circus resounds. If not in arms, you are in tongue at all events always rebellious. But I suppose it is quite another affair to refuse to swear by the genius of Cæsar? For it is fairly open to doubt as to who are perjurers on this point, when you do not swear honestly even by your gods. Well, we do not call the emperor God; for on this point *sannam facimus*, as the saying is. But the truth is, that you who call Cæsar God both mock him, by calling him what he is not, and curse him, because he does not want to be what you call him. For he prefers living to being made a god.

Chapter XVIII.—Christians Charged with an Obstinate Contempt of Death. Instances of the Same are Found Amongst the Heathen.

The rest of your charge of obstinacy against us you sum up in this indictment, that we boldly refuse neither your swords, nor your crosses, nor your wild beasts, nor fire, nor tortures, such is our obduracy and contempt of death. But (you are inconsistent in your charges); for in former times amongst your own ancestors all these terrors have come in men's intrepidity not only to be despised, but even to be held in great praise. How many swords there were, and what brave men were willing to suffer by them, it were irksome to enumerate. (If we take the torture) of the cross, of which so many instances have occurred, exquisite in cruelty, your own Regulus readily initiated the suffering which up to his day was without a precedent; a queen of Egypt used wild beasts of her own (to accomplish her death); the Carthaginian woman, who in the last extremity of her country was more courageous than her husband Asdrubal, only followed the example, set long before by Dido herself, of going through fire to her death. Then, again, a woman of Athens defied the tyrant, exhausted his tortures, and at last, lest her person and sex might succumb through weakness, she bit off her tongue and spat out of her mouth the only possible instrument of a confession which was now out of her power. But in your own instance you account such deeds glorious, in ours obstinate. Annihilate now the glory of your ancestors, in order that you may thereby annihilate us also. Be content from henceforth to repeal the praises of your forefathers, in order that you may not have to accord commendation to us for the same (sufferings). Perhaps (you will say) the character of a more robust age may have rendered the spirits of antiquity more enduring. Now, however, (we enjoy) the blessing of quietness and peace; so that the minds and dispositions of men (should be) more tolerant even towards strangers. Well, you rejoin, be it so: *you* may compare *yourselves* with the ancients; *we* must needs pursue with hatred all that we find in you offensive to *ourselves*, because it does not obtain currency among us. Answer me, then, on each particular case by itself. I am not seeking for examples on a uniform scale. Since, forsooth, the sword through their contempt of death produced stories of heroism amongst your ancestors, it is not, of course, from love of life that you go to the trainers sword in hand and offer yourselves as gladiators, (nor) through fear of death do you enroll your names in the army. Since an ordinary woman makes her death famous by wild beasts, it cannot but be of your own pure accord that you encounter wild beasts day after day in the midst of peaceful times. Although no longer any Regulus among you has raised a cross as the instrument of his own crucifixion, yet a contempt of the fire has even now displayed itself, since one of yourselves very lately has offered for a wager to go to any place which may be fixed upon and put on the burning shirt. If a woman once defiantly danced beneath the scourge, the same feat has been very recently performed again by one of your own (circus-) hunters as he traversed the appointed course, not to mention the famous sufferings of the Spartans.

Chapter XIX.—If Christians and the Heathen Thus Resemble Each Other, There is Great Difference in the Grounds and Nature of Their Apparently Similar Conduct.

Here end, I suppose, your tremendous charges of obstinacy against the Christians. Now, since we are amenable to them in common with yourselves, it only remains that we compare the grounds which the respective parties have for being personally derided. All our obstinacy, however, is with you a foregone conclusion, based on our strong convictions; for we take for granted a resurrection of the dead. Hope in this resurrection amounts to a contempt of death. Ridicule, therefore, as much as you like the excessive stupidity of such minds as die that they may live; but then, in order that you may be able to laugh more merrily, and deride us with greater boldness, you must take your sponge, or perhaps your tongue, and wipe away those records of yours every now and then cropping out, which assert in not dissimilar terms that souls will return to bodies. But how much more worthy of acceptance is our belief which maintains that they will return to the same bodies! And how much more ridiculous is your inherited conceit, that the human spirit is to reappear in a dog, or a mule, or a peacock! Again, we affirm that a judgment has been ordained by God according to the merits of every man. This you ascribe to Minos and Rhadamanthus, while at the same time *you* reject Aristides, who was a juster judge than either. By the award of the judgment, we say that the wicked will have to spend an eternity in endless fire, the pious and innocent in a region of bliss. In your view likewise an unalterable condition is ascribed to the respective destinations of Pyriphlegethon and Elysium. Now they are not merely your composers of myth and poetry who write songs of this strain; but your philosophers also speak with all confidence of the return of souls to their former state, and of the twofold award of a final judgment.

Chapter XX.—Truth and Reality Pertain to Christians Alone. The Heathen Counseled to Examine and Embrace It.

How long therefore, O most unjust heathen, will you refuse to acknowledge us, and (what is more) to execrate your own (worthies), since between us no distinction has place, because we are one and the same? Since you do not (of course) hate what you yourselves are, give us rather your right hands in fellowship, unite your salutations, mingle your embraces, sanguinary with the sanguinary, incestuous with the incestuous, conspirators with conspirators, obstinate and vain with those of the selfsame qualities. In company with each other, we have been traitors to the majesty of the gods; and together do we provoke their indignation. You too have your "third race;" not indeed third in the way of religious rite, but a third race in sex, and, made up as it is of male and female in one, it is more fitted to men and women (for offices of lust). Well, then, do we offend you by the very fact of our approximation and agreement? Being on a par is apt to furnish unconsciously the materials for rivalry. Thus "a potter envies a potter, and a smith a smith." But we must now discontinue this imaginary confession. Our conscience has returned to the truth, and to the consistency of truth. For all those points which you allege (against us) will be really found in ourselves alone; and we alone can rebut them, against whom they are adduced, by getting you to listen to the other side of the question, whence that full knowledge is learnt which both inspires counsel and directs the judgment. Now it is in fact your own maxim, that no one should determine a cause without hearing both sides of it; and it is only in our own case that you neglect (the equitable principle). You indulge to the Full that fault of human nature, that those things which you do not disallow in yourselves you condemn in others, or you boldly charge against others those things the guilt of which you retain a lasting consciousness of770 in yourselves. The course of life in which you will choose to occupy yourselves is different from ours: whilst chaste in the eyes of others, you are unchaste towards your own selves; whilst vigorous against vice out of doors, you succumb to it at home. This is the injustice (which we have to suffer), that, knowing truth, we are condemned by those who know it not; free from guilt, we are judged by those who are implicated in it. Remove the mote, or rather the beam, out of your own eye, that you may be able to extract the mote from the eyes of others. Amend your own lives first, that you may be able to punish the Christians. Only so far as you shall have effected your own reformation, will you refuse to inflict punishment on them—nay, so far will you have become Christians yourselves; and as you shall have become Christians, so far will you have compassed your own amendment of life. Learn what that is which you accuse in us, and you will accuse no longer; search out what that is which you do not accuse in yourselves, and you will become self-accusers. From these very few and humble remarks, so far as we have been able to open out the subject to you, you will plainly get some insight into (your own) error, and some discovery of *our* truth. Condemn that truth if you have the heart, but only after you have examined it; and approve the error still, if you are so minded, only first explore it. But if your prescribed rule is to love error and hate truth, why, (let me ask,) do you not probe to a full discovery the objects both of your love and your hatred?

Book II.

Chapter I.—The Heathen Gods from Heathen Authorities. Varro Has Written a Work on the Subject. His Threefold Classification. The Changeable Character of that Which Ought to Be Fixed and Certain.

Our defense requires that we should at this point discuss with you the character of your gods, O ye heathen, fit objects of our pity, appealing even to your own conscience to determine whether they be truly gods, as you would have it supposed, or falsely, as you are unwilling to have proved. Now this is the material part of human error, owing to the wiles of its author, that it is never free from the ignorance of error, whence your guilt is all the greater. Your eyes are open, yet they see not; your ears are unstopped, yet they hear not; though your heart beats, it is yet dull, nor does your mind understand that of which it is cognizant. If indeed the enormous perverseness (of your worship) could be broken up by a single demurrer, we should have our objection ready to hand in the declaration that, as we know all those gods of yours to have been instituted by men, all belief in the true Deity is by this very circumstance brought to naught; because, of course, nothing which some time or other had a beginning can rightly seem to be divine. But the fact is, there are many things by which tenderness of conscience is hardened into the callousness of willful error. Truth is beleaguered with the vast force (of the enemy), and yet how secure she is in her own inherent strength! And naturally enough when from her very adversaries she gains to her side whomsoever she will, as her friends and protectors, and prostrates the entire host of her assailants. It is therefore against these things that our contest lies—against the institutions of our ancestors, against the authority of tradition, the laws of our governors, and the reasonings of the wise; against antiquity, custom, submission; against precedents, prodigies, miracles,—all which things have had their part in consolidating that spurious system of your gods. Wishing, then, to follow step by step your own commentaries which you have drawn out of your theology of every sort (because the authority of learned men goes further with you in matters of this kind than the testimony of facts), I have taken and abridged the works of Varro; for he in his treatise *Concerning Divine Things*, collected out of ancient digests, has shown himself a serviceable guide for us. Now, if I inquire of him who were the subtle inventors of the gods, he points to either the philosophers, the peoples, or the poets. For he has made a threefold distinction in classifying the gods: one being the *physical* class, of which the philosophers treat; another the *mythic* class, which is the constant burden of the poets; the third, the *gentile* class, which the nations have adopted each one for itself. When, therefore, the philosophers have ingeniously composed their physical (theology) out of their own conjectures, when the poets have drawn their mythical from fables, and the (several) nations have forged their gentile (polytheism) according to their own will, where in the world must truth be placed? In the conjectures? Well, but these are only a doubtful conception. In the fables? But they are at best an absurd story. In the popular accounts? This sort of opinion, however, is only promiscuous and municipal. Now all things with the philosophers are uncertain, because of their variation with the poets all is worthless, because immoral; with the nations all is irregular and confused, because dependent on their mere choice. The nature of God, however, if it be the true one with which you are concerned, is of so definite a character as not to be derived from uncertain speculations, nor contaminated with worthless fables, nor determined by promiscuous conceits. It ought indeed to be regarded, as it really is, as certain, entire, universal, because it is in truth the property of all. Now, what god shall I believe? One that has been gauged by vague suspicion? One that history has divulged? One that a community has invented? It would be a far worthier thing if I believed no god, than one which is open to doubt, or full of shame, or the object of arbitrary selection.

Chapter II.—Philosophers Had Not Succeeded in Discovering God. The Uncertainty and Confusion of Their Speculations.

But the authority of the physical philosophers is maintained *among you* as the special property of wisdom. *You mean* of course, that pure and simple wisdom of the philosophers which attests its own weakness mainly by that variety of opinion which proceeds from an ignorance of the truth. Now what wise man is so devoid of truth, as not to know that God is the Father and Lord of wisdom itself and truth? Besides, there is that divine oracle uttered by Solomon: "The fear of the Lord," says he, "is the beginning of wisdom." But fear has its origin in knowledge; for how will a man fear that of which he knows nothing? Therefore he who shall have the fear of God, even if he be ignorant of all things else, if he has attained to the knowledge and truth of God, will possess full and perfect wisdom. This, however, is what philosophy has not clearly realized. For although, in their inquisitive disposition to search into all kinds of learning, *the philosophers* may seem to have investigated the sacred Scriptures themselves for their antiquity, and to have derived thence some of their opinions; yet because they have interpolated *these deductions* they prove that they have either despised them wholly or have not fully believed them, for in other cases also the simplicity of truth is shaken by the over-scrupulousness of an irregular belief, and that they therefore changed them, as their desire of glory grew, into products of their own mind. The consequence of this is, that even that which they had discovered degenerated into uncertainty, and there arose from one or two drops of truth a perfect flood of argumentation. For after they had simply found God, they did not expound Him as they found Him, but rather disputed about His quality, and His nature, and even about His abode. The Platonists, indeed, (held) Him to care about worldly things, both as the disposer and judge thereof. The Epicureans *regarded* Him as apathetic and inert, and (so to say) a nonentity. The Stoics believed Him to be outside of the world; the Platonists, within the world. The God whom they had so imperfectly admitted, they could neither know nor fear; and therefore they could not be wise, since they wandered away indeed from the beginning of wisdom," that is, "the fear of God." Proofs are not wanting that among the philosophers there was not only an ignorance, but actual doubt, about the divinity. Diogenes, when asked what was taking place in heaven, answered by saying, "I have never been up there." Again, whether there were any gods, he replied, "I do not know; only there ought to be gods." When Croesus inquired of Thales of Miletus what he thought of the gods, the latter having taken some time to consider, answered by the word "Nothing." Even Socrates denied with an air of certainty those gods of yours. Yet he with a like certainty requested that a cock should be sacrificed to Æsculapius. And therefore when philosophy, in its practice of defining about God, is detected in such uncertainty and inconsistency, what "fear" could it possibly have had of Him whom it was not competent clearly to determine? We have been taught to believe of the world that it is god. For such the physical class of theologizers conclude it to be, since they have handed down such views about the gods that Dionysius the Stoic divides them into three kinds. The first, he supposes, includes those gods which are most obvious, as the Sun, Moon, *and* Stars; the next, those which are not apparent, as Neptune; the remaining one, those which are said to have passed from the human state to the divine, as Hercules *and* Amphiaraus. In like manner, Arcesilaus makes a threefold form of the divinity—the Olympian, the Astral, the Titanian—sprung from Coelus and Terra; from which through Saturn and Ops came Neptune, Jupiter, and Orcus, and their entire progeny. Xenocrates, of the Academy, makes a twofold division—the Olympian and the Titanian, which descend from Coelus and Terra. Most of the Egyptians believe that there are four gods—the Sun and the Moon, the Heaven and the Earth. Along with all the supernal fire Democritus conjectures that the gods arose. Zeno, too, will have it that their nature resembles it. Whence Varro also makes fire to be the soul of the world, that in the world fire governs all things, just as the soul does in ourselves. But all this is most absurd. For he says,

Whilst it is in us, we have existence; but as soon as it has left us, we die. Therefore, when fire quits the world in lightning, the world comes to its end.

Chapter III.—The Physical Philosophers Maintained the Divinity of the Elements; The Absurdity of the Tenet Exposed.

From these developments of opinion, we see that your physical class *of philosophers* are driven to the necessity of contending that the elements are gods, since it alleges that other gods are sprung from them; for it is only from gods that gods could be born. Now, although we shall have to examine these other gods more fully in the proper place, in the mythic section of the poets, yet, inasmuch as we must meanwhile treat of them in their connection with the present class, we shall probably even from their present class, when once we turn to the gods themselves, succeed in showing that they can by no means appear to be gods who are said to be sprung from the elements; so that we have at once a presumption that the elements are not gods, since they which are born of the elements are not gods. In like manner, whilst we show that the elements are not gods, we shall, according to the law of natural relationship, get a presumptive argument that they cannot rightly be maintained to be gods whose parents (in this case the elements) are not gods. It is a settled point that a god is born of a god, and that what lacks divinity is born of what is not divine. Now, so far as the world of which your philosophers treat (for I apply this term to the *universe* in the most comprehensive sense) contains the elements, ministering to them as its component parts (for whatever its own condition may be, the same of course will be that of its elements and constituent portions), it must needs have been formed either by some being, according to the enlightened view of Plato, or else by none, according to the harsh opinion of Epicurus; and since it was formed, by having a beginning, it must also have an end. That, therefore, which at one time before its beginning had no existence, and will by and by after its end cease to have an existence, cannot of course, by any possibility, seem to be a god, wanting as it does that essential character of divinity, eternity, which is reckoned to be without beginning, and without end. If, however, it is in no wise formed, and therefore ought to be accounted divine—since, as divine, it is subject neither to a beginning nor an end of itself—how is it that some assign generation to the elements, which they hold to be gods, when the Stoics deny that anything can be born of a god? Likewise, how is it that they wish those beings, whom they suppose to be born of the elements, to be regarded as gods, when they deny that a god can be born? Now, what must hold good of the universe will have to be predicated of the elements, I mean of heaven, and of earth, and of the stars, and of fire, which Varro has vainly proposed that you should believe to be gods, and the parents of gods, contrary to that generation and nativity which he had declared to be impossible in a god. Now this same Varro had shown that the earth and the stars were animated. But if this be the case, they must needs be also mortal, according to the condition of animated nature; for although the soul is evidently immortal, this attribute is limited to it alone: it is not extended to that with which it is associated, that is, the body. Nobody, however, will deny that the elements have body, since we both touch them and are touched by them, and we see certain bodies fall down from them. If, therefore, they are animated, laying aside the principle of a soul, as befits their condition as bodies, they are mortal—of course not immortal. And yet whence is it that the elements appear to Varro to be animated? Because, forsooth, the elements have motion. And then, in order to anticipate what may be objected on the other side, that many things else have motion—as wheels, as carriages, as several other machines—he volunteers the statement that he believes only such things to be animated as move of themselves, without any apparent mover or impeller from without, like the apparent mover of the wheel, or propeller of the carriage, or director of the machine. If, then, they are not animated, they have no motion of themselves. Now, when he thus alleges a power which is not apparent, he points to what it was his duty to seek after, even the creator and controller of the motion; for it does not at once follow that, because we do not see a thing, we believe that it does not exist. Rather, it is necessary the more profoundly to investigate what one does not see, in order the better to understand the character of that which is apparent. Besides if (you admit) only the existence of those things which appear and are supposed to exist simply because they appear, how is it that you also admit them to be gods which do not appear? If, moreover, those things seem to have existence which have none, why may they not have existence also which do not seem to have it? Such, for instance, as the Mover of the heavenly beings. Granted, then, that things are animated because they move of themselves, and that they move of themselves when they are not moved by another: still it does not follow that they must straightway be gods, because they are animated, nor even because they move of themselves; else what is to prevent all animals whatever being accounted gods, moving as they do of themselves? This, to be sure, is allowed to the Egyptians, but their *superstitious* vanity has another basis.

Chapter IV.—Wrong Derivation of the Word Θεός. The Name Indicative of the True Deity. God Without Shape and Immaterial. Anecdote of Thales.

Some affirm that the gods (*i.e.* θεοί) were so called because the verbs θέειν and σείσθαι signify *to run* and *to be moved*. This term, then, is not indicative of any majesty, for it is derived from running and motion, not from any dominion of godhead. But inasmuch as the Supreme God whom we worship is also designated Θεός, without however the appearance of any *course* or *motion* in Him, because He is not visible to any one, it is clear that that word must have had some other derivation, and that the property of divinity, innate in Himself, must have been discovered. Dismissing, then, that ingenious interpretation, it is more likely that the gods were not called θεοί from *running* and *motion*, but that the term was borrowed from the designation of the true God; so that you gave the name θεοί to the gods, whom you had in like manner forged for yourselves. Now, that this is the case, a plain proof is afforded in the fact that you actually give the common appellation θεοί to all those gods of yours, in whom there is no attribute of *course* or *motion* indicated. When, therefore, you call them both θεοί and *immoveable* with equal readiness, there is a deviation as well from the meaning of the word as from the idea of godhead, which is set aside if measured by the notion of *course* and *motion*. But if that *sacred* name be peculiarly significant of deity, and be simply true and not of a forced interpretation in the case of the *true* God, but transferred in a borrowed sense to those other objects which you choose to call gods, then you ought to show to us that there is also a community of character between them, so that their common designation may rightly depend on their union of essence. But the true God, on the sole ground that He is not an object of sense, is incapable of being compared with those false deities which are cognizable to sight and sense (to sense indeed is sufficient); for this amounts to a clear statement of the difference between an obscure proof and a manifest one. Now, since the elements are obvious to all, (and) since God, on the contrary, is visible to none, how will it be in your power from that part which you have not seen to pass to a decision on the objects which you see? Since, therefore, you have not to combine them in your perception or your reason, why do you combine them in name with the purpose of combining them also in power? For see how even Zeno separates the matter of the world from God: he says that the latter has percolated through the former, like honey through the comb. God, therefore, and Matter are two words (and) two things. Proportioned to the difference of the words is the diversity of the things; the condition also of matter follows its designation. Now if matter is not God, because its very appellation teaches us so, how can those things which are inherent in matter—that is, the elements—be regarded as gods, since the component members cannot possibly be heterogeneous from the body? But what concern have I with physiological conceits? It were better for one's mind to ascend above the state of the world, not to stoop down to uncertain speculations. Plato's form for the world was round. Its square, angular shape, such as others had conceived it to be, he rounded off, I suppose, with compasses, from his laboring to have it believed to be simply without a beginning. Epicurus, however, who had said, "What is above us is nothing to us," wished notwithstanding to have a peep at the sky, and found the sun to be a foot in diameter. Thus far you must confess men were niggardly in even celestial objects. In process of time their ambitious conceptions advanced, and so the sun too enlarged its disk. Accordingly, the Peripatetics marked it out as a larger world. Now, pray tell me, what wisdom is there in this hankering after conjectural speculations? What proof is afforded to us, notwithstanding the strong confidence of its assertions, by the useless affectation of a scrupulous curiosity, which is tricked out with an artful show of language? It therefore served Thales of Miletus quite right, when, star-gazing as he walked with all the eyes he had, he had the mortification of falling into a well, and was unmercifully twitted by an Egyptian, who said to him, "Is it because you found nothing on earth to look at, that you think you ought to confine your gaze to the sky?" His fall, therefore, is a figurative picture of the philosophers; of those, I mean, who persist in applying their studies to a vain purpose, since they indulge a stupid curiosity on natural objects, which they ought rather (intelligently to direct) to their Creator and Governor.

Chapter V.—The Physical Theory Continued. Further Reasons Advanced Against the Divinity of the Elements.

Why, then, do we not resort to that far more reasonable opinion, which has clear proof of being derived from men's common sense and unsophisticated deduction? Even Varro bears it in mind, when he says that the elements are supposed to be divine, because nothing whatever is capable, without their concurrence, of being produced, nourished, or applied to the sustenance of man's life and of the earth, since not even our bodies and souls could have sufficed in themselves without the modification of the elements. By this it is that the world is made generally habitable,—a result which is harmoniously secured by the distribution into zones, except where human residence has been rendered impracticable by intensity of cold or heat. On this account, men have accounted as gods—the sun, because it imparts from itself the light of day, ripens the fruit with its warmth, and measures the year with its stated periods; the moon, which is at once the solace of the night and the controller of the months by its governance; the stars also, certain indications as they are of those seasons which are to be observed in the tillage of our fields; lastly, the very heaven also under which, and the earth over which, as well as the intermediate space within which, all things conspire together for the good of man. Nor is it from their beneficent influences only that a faith in their divinity has been deemed compatible with the elements, but from their opposite qualities also, such as usually happen from what one might call their wrath and anger—as thunder, and hail, and drought, and pestilential winds, floods also, and openings of the ground, and earthquakes: these are all fairly enough accounted gods, whether their nature becomes the object of reverence as being favorable, or of fear because terrible—the sovereign dispenser, in fact, both of help and of hurt. But in the practical conduct of social life, this is the way in which men act and feel: they do not show gratitude or find fault with the very things from which the succor or the injury proceeds, so much as with them by whose strength and power the operation of the things is affected. For even in your amusements you do not award the crown as a prize to the flute or the harp, but to the musician who manages the said flute or harp by the power of his delightful skill. In like manner, when one is in ill-health, you do not bestow your acknowledgments on the flannel wraps, or the medicines, or the poultices, but on the doctors by whose care and prudence the remedies become effectual. So again, in untoward events, they who are wounded with the sword do not charge the injury on the sword or the spear, but on the enemy or the robber; whilst those whom a falling house covers do not blame the tiles or the stones, but the oldness of the building; as again shipwrecked sailors impute their calamity not to the rocks and waves, but to the tempest. And rightly too; for it is certain that everything which happens must be ascribed not to the instrument with which, but to the agent by whom, it takes place; inasmuch as he is the prime cause of the occurrence,[863] who appoints both the event itself and that by whose instrumentality it comes to pass (as there are in all things these three particular elements—the fact itself, its instrument, and its cause), because he himself who wills the occurrence of a thing comes into notice prior to the thing which he wills, or the instrument by which it occurs. On all other occasions therefore, your conduct is right enough, because you consider the author; but in physical phenomena your rule is opposed to that natural principle which prompts you to a wise judgment in all other cases, removing out of sight as you do the supreme position of the author, and considering rather the things that happen, than him by whom they happen. Thus it comes to pass that you suppose the power and the dominion to belong to the elements, which are but the slaves and functionaries. Now do we not, in thus tracing out an artificer and master within, expose the artful structure of their slavery out of the appointed functions of those elements to which you ascribe (the attributes) of power?[866] But gods are not slaves; therefore whatever things are servile in character are not gods. Otherwise they should prove to us that, according to the ordinary course of things, liberty is promoted by irregular license, despotism by liberty, and that by despotism divine power is meant. For if all the (heavenly bodies) overhead forget not to fulfill their courses in certain orbits, in regular seasons, at proper distances, *and* at equal intervals—appointed in the way of a law for the revolutions of time, and for directing the guidance thereof—can it fail to result from the very observance of their conditions and the fidelity of their operations, that you will be convinced both by the recurrence of their orbital courses and the accuracy of their mutations, when you bear in mind how ceaseless is their recurrence, that a governing power presides over them, to which the entire management of the world is obedient, reaching even to the utility and injury of the human race? For you cannot pretend that these (phenomena) act and care for themselves alone, without contributing anything to the advantage of mankind, when you maintain that the elements are divine for no other reason than that you experience from them either benefit or injury to yourself. For if they benefit themselves only, you are under no obligation to them.

Chapter VI.—The Changes of the Heavenly Bodies, Proof that They are Not Divine. Transition from the Physical to the Mythic Class of Gods.

Come now, do you allow that the Divine Being not only has nothing servile in His course, but exists in unimpaired integrity, and ought not to be diminished, or suspended, or destroyed? Well, then, all His blessedness would disappear, if He were ever subject to change. Look, however, at the stellar bodies; they both undergo change, and give clear evidence of the fact. The moon tells us how great has been its loss, as it recovers its full form; its greater losses you are already accustomed to measure in a mirror of water; so that I need not any longer believe in any wise what magians have asserted. The sun, too, is frequently put to the trial of an eclipse. Explain as best you may the modes of these celestial casualties, it is impossible for God either to become less or to cease to exist.

Vain, therefore, are those supports of human learning, which, by their artful method of weaving conjectures, belie both wisdom and truth. Besides, it so happens, indeed, according to your natural way of thinking, that he who has spoken the best is supposed to have spoken most truly, instead of him who has spoken the truth being held to have spoken the best. Now the man who shall carefully look into things, will surely allow it to be a greater probability that those elements which we have been discussing are under some rule and direction, than that they have a motion of their own, and that being under government they cannot be gods. If, however, one is in error in this matter, it is better to err simply than speculatively, like your physical philosophers. But, at the same time, if you consider the character of the *mythic* school, (and compare it with the *physical*,) the error which we have already seen frail men making in the latter is really the more respectable one, since it ascribes a divine nature to those things which it supposes to be *superhuman* in their sensibility, whether in respect of their position, their power, their magnitude, or their divinity. For that which you suppose to be higher than man, you believe to be very near to God.

Chapter VII.—The Gods of the Mythic Class. The Poets a Very Poor Authority in Such Matters. Homer and the Mythic Poets. Why Irreligious.

But to pass to the *mythic* class of gods, which we attributed to the poets, I hardly know whether I must only seek to put them on a par with our own *human* mediocrity, or whether they must be affirmed to be gods, with proofs of divinity, like the African Mopsus and the Boeotian Amphiaraus. I must now indeed but slightly touch on this class, of which a fuller view will be taken in the proper place. Meanwhile, that these were only human beings, is clear from the fact that you do not consistently call them gods, but heroes. Why then discuss the point? Although divine honors had to be ascribed to dead men, it was not to them as such, of course. Look at your own practice, when with similar excess of presumption you sully heaven with the sepulchers of your kings: is it not such as are illustrious for justice, virtue, piety, and every excellence of this sort, that you honor with the blessedness of deification, contented even to incur contempt if you forswear yourselves for such characters? And, on the other hand, do you not deprive the impious and disgraceful of even the old prizes of human glory, tear up their decrees and titles, pull down their statues, and deface their images on the current coin? Will He, however, who beholds all things, who approves, nay, rewards the good, prostitute before all men the attribute of His own inexhaustible grace and mercy? And shall men be allowed an especial mount of care and righteousness, that they may be wise in selecting and multiplying their deities? Shall attendants on kings and princes be more pure than those who wait on the Supreme God? You turn your back in horror, indeed, on outcasts and exiles, on the poor and weak, on the obscurely born and the low-lived; but yet you honor, even by legal sanctions, unchaste men, adulterers, robbers, and parricides. Must we regard it as a subject of ridicule or indignation, that such characters are believed to be gods who are not fit to be men? Then, again, in this mythic class of yours which the poets celebrate, how uncertain is your conduct as to purity of conscience and the maintenance thereof! For whenever we hold up to execration the wretched, disgraceful and atrocious (examples) of your gods, you defend them as mere fables, on the pretence of poetic license; whenever we volunteer a silent contempt of this said poetic *license*, then you are not only troubled with no horror of it, but you go so far as to show it respect, and to hold it as one of the indispensable (fine) arts; nay, you carry out the studies of your higher classes by its means, as the very foundation of your literature. Plato was of opinion that poets ought to be banished, as calumniators of the gods; (he would even have) Homer himself expelled from his republic, although, as you are aware, he was the crowned head of them all. But while you admit and retain them thus, why should you not believe them when they disclose such things respecting your gods? And if you do believe your poets, how is it that you worship such gods (as they describe)? If you worship them simply because you do not believe the poets, why do you bestow praise on such lying authors, without any fear of giving offence to those whose calumniators you honor? A regard for truth is not, of course, to be expected of poets. But when you say that they only make men into gods after their death, do you not admit that before death the said gods were merely human? Now what is there strange in the fact, that they who were once men are subject to the dishonor of human casualties, or crimes, or fables? Do you not, in fact, put faith in your poets, when it is in accordance with their rhapsodies that you have arranged in some instances your very rituals? How is it that the priestess of Ceres is ravished, if it is not because Ceres suffered a similar outrage? Why are the children of others sacrificed to Saturn, if it is not because he spared not his own? Why is a male mutilated in honor of the Idæan goddess *Cybele*, unless it be that the (unhappy) youth who was too disdainful of her advances was castrated, owing to her vexation at his daring to cross her love? Why was not Hercules "a dainty dish" to the good ladies of Lanuvium, if it was not for the primeval offence which women gave to him? The poets, no doubt, are liars. Yet it is not because *of their telling us that* your gods did such things when they were human beings, nor because they predicated divine scandals of a divine state, since it seemed to you more credible that gods should exist, though not of such a character, than that there should be such characters, although not gods.

Chapter VIII.—The Gods of the Different Nations. Varro's Gentile Class. Their Inferiority. A Good Deal of This Perverse Theology Taken from Scripture. Serapis a Perversion of Joseph.

There remains the *gentile* class of gods amongst the several nations: these were adopted out of mere caprice, not from the knowledge of the truth; and our information about them comes from the private notions *of different races*. God, I imagine, is everywhere known, everywhere present, powerful everywhere—an object whom all ought to worship, all ought to serve. Since, then, it happens that even they, whom all the world worships in common, fail in the evidence of their true divinity, how much more must this befall those whom their very votaries have not succeeded in discovering! For what useful authority could possibly precede a theology of so defective a character as to be wholly unknown to fame? How many have either seen or heard of the Syrian Atargatis, the African Coelestis, the Moorish Varsutina, the Arabian Obodas and Dusaris, or the Norican Belenus, or those whom Varro mentions—Deluentinus of Casinum, Visidianus of Narnia, Numiternus of Atina, *or* Anchariaof Asculum? And who have any clear notions of Nortia of Vulsinii? There is no difference in the worth of even their names, apart from the human surnames which distinguish them. I laugh often enough at the little coteries of gods in each municipality, which have their honors confined within their own city walls. To what lengths this license of adopting gods has been pushed, the superstitious practices of the Egyptians show us; for they worship even their native animals, *such as* cats, crocodiles, and their snake. It is therefore a small matter that they have also deified a man— him, I mean, whom not Egypt only, or Greece, but the whole world worships, and the Africans swear by; about whose state also all that helps our conjectures and imparts to our knowledge the semblance of truth is stated in our own (sacred) literature. For that Serapis of yours was originally one of our own saints called Joseph. The youngest of his brethren, but superior to them in intellect, he was from envy sold into Egypt, and became a slave in the family of Pharaoh king of the country. Importuned by the unchaste queen, when he refused to comply with her desire, she turned upon him and reported him to the king, by whom he is put into prison. There he displays the power of his divine inspiration, by interpreting aright the dreams of some (fellow-prisoners).Meanwhile the king, too, has some terrible dreams. Joseph being brought before him, according to his summons, was able to expound them. Having narrated the proofs of true interpretation which he had given in the prison, he opens out his dream to the king: those seven fat-fleshed and well-favored kine signified as many years of plenty; in like manner, the seven lean-fleshed animals predicted the scarcity of the seven following years. He accordingly recommends precautions to be taken against the future famine from the previous plenty. The king believed him. The issue of all that happened showed how wise he was, how invariably holy, and now how necessary. So Pharaoh set him over all Egypt, that he might secure the provision of corn for it, and thenceforth administer its government. They called him Serapis, from the turban which adorned his head. The peck-like shape of this turban marks the memory of his corn-provisioning; whilst evidence is given that the care of the supplies was all on his head, by the very ears of corn which embellish the border of the head-dress. For the same reason, also, they made the sacred figure of a dog, which they regard (as a sentry) in Hades, and put it under his right hand, because the care of the Egyptians was concentrated under his hand. And they put at his side Pharia, whose name shows her to have been the king's daughter. For in addition to all the rest of his kind gifts and rewards, Pharaoh had given him his own daughter in marriage. Since, however, they had begun to worship both wild animals and human beings, they combined both figures under one form Anubis, in which there may rather be seen clear proofs of its own character and condition enshrined by a nation at war with itself, refractory to its kings, despised among foreigners, with even the appetite of a slave and the filthy nature of a dog.

Chapter IX.—The Power of Rome. Romanized Aspect of All the Heathen Mythology. Varro's Threefold Distribution Criticized. Roman Heroes (Æneas Included,) Unfavorably Reviewed.

Such are the more obvious or more remarkable points which we had to mention in connection with Varro's threefold distribution of the gods, in order that a sufficient answer might seem to be given touching the physical, the poetic, and the gentile classes. Since, however, it is no longer to the philosophers, nor the poets, nor the nations that we owe the substitution of all (heathen worship for the true religion) although they transmitted the superstition, but to the dominant Romans, who received the tradition and gave it wide authority, another phase of the widespread error of man must now be encountered by us; nay, another forest must be felled *by our axe*, which has obscured the childhood of the degenerate worship with germs of superstitions gathered from all quarters. Well, but even the gods of the Romans have received from (the same) Varro a threefold classification into the *certain*, the *uncertain*, and the *select*. What absurdity! What need had they of uncertain gods, when they possessed certain ones? Unless, forsooth, they wished to commit themselves to such folly as the Athenians did; for at Athens there was an altar with this inscription: "To the unknown gods." Does, then, a man worship that which he knows nothing of? Then, again, as they had certain gods, they ought to have been contented with them, without requiring select ones. In this want they are even found to be irreligious! For if gods are selected as onions are, then such as are not chosen are declared to be worthless. Now we on our part allow that the Romans had two sets of gods, *common* and *proper*; in other words, those which they had in common with other nations, and those which they themselves devised.

And were not these called the *public* and the *foreign* gods? Their altars tell us so; there is (a specimen) of the foreign gods at the fane of Carna, of the public gods in the Palatium. Now, since their common gods are comprehended in both the physical and the mythic classes, we have already said enough concerning them. I should like to speak of their particular kinds of deity. We ought then to admire the Romans for that third set of *the gods of their enemies*, because no other nation ever discovered for itself so large a mass of superstition. Their other deities we arrange in two classes: those which have become gods from human beings, and those which have had their origin in some other way. Now, since there is advanced the same colorable pretext for the deification of the dead, that their lives were meritorious, we are compelled to urge the same reply against them, that no one of them was worth so much pains. Their fond father Æneas, in whom they believed, was never glorious, and was felled with a stone—a vulgar weapon, to pelt a dog withal, inflicting a wound no less ignoble! But this Æneas turns out a traitor to his country; yes, quite as much as Antenor. And if they will not believe this to be true of him, he at any rate deserted his companions when his country was in flames, and must be held inferior to that woman of Carthage, who, when her husband Hasdrubal supplicated the enemy with the mild pusillanimity of our Æneas, refused to accompany him, but hurrying her children along with her, disdained to take her beautiful self and father's noble heart into exile, but plunged into the flames of the burning Carthage, as if rushing into the embraces of her (dear but) ruined country. Is he "pious Æneas" for (rescuing) his young only son and decrepit old father, but deserting Priam and Astyanax? But the Romans ought rather to detest him; for in defense of their princes and their royal house, they surrender even children and wives, and every dearest pledge. They deify the son of Venus, and this with the full knowledge and consent of *her husband* Vulcan, and without opposition from even Juno. Now, if sons have seats in heaven owing to their piety to their parents, why are not those noble youths of Argos rather accounted gods, because they, to save their mother from guilt in the performance of some sacred rites, with a devotion more than human, yoked themselves to her car and dragged her to the temple? Why not make a goddess, for her exceeding piety, of that daughter who from her own breasts nourished her father who was famishing in prison? What other glorious achievement can be related of Æneas, but that he was nowhere seen in the fight on the field of Laurentum? Following his bent, perhaps he fled a second time as a fugitive from the battle. In like manner, Romulus posthumously becomes a god. Was it because he founded the city? Then why not others also, who have built cities, counting even women? To be sure, Romulus slew his brother in the bargain, and trickishly ravished some foreign virgins. Therefore of course he becomes a god, and therefore a Quirinus ("god of the spear"), because then their fathers had to use the spear on his account. What did Sterculus do to merit deification? If he worked hard to enrich the fields *stercoribus*, (with manure,) Augias had more dung than he to bestow on them. If Faunus, the son of Picus, used to do violence to law and right, because struck with madness, it was more fit that he should be doctored than deified. If the daughter of Faunus so excelled in chastity, that she would hold no conversation with men, it was perhaps from rudeness, or a consciousness of deformity, or shame for her father's insanity. How much worthier of divine honor than this "good goddess" was Penelope, who, although dwelling among so many suitors of the vilest character, preserved with delicate tact the purity which they assailed! There is Sanctus, too, who for his hospitality had a temple consecrated to him by king Plotius; and even Ulysses had it in his power to have bestowed one more god upon you in the person of the most refined Alcinous.

Chapter X.—A Disgraceful Feature of the Roman Mythology. It Honors Such Infamous Characters as Larentina.

I hasten to even more abominable cases. Your writers have not been ashamed to publish that of Larentina. She was a hired prostitute, whether as the nurse of Romulus, and therefore called *Lupa*, because she was a prostitute, or as the mistress of Hercules, now deceased, that is to say, now deified. They relate that his temple-warder happened to be playing at dice in the temple alone; and in order to represent a partner for himself in the game, in the absence of an actual one, he began to play with one hand for Hercules and the other for himself. (The condition was,) that if he won the stakes from Hercules, he should with them procure a supper and a prostitute; if Hercules, however, proved the winner, I mean his other hand, then he should provide the same for Hercules. The hand of Hercules won. That achievement might well have been added to his twelve labors! The temple-warden buys a supper for the hero, and hires Larentina to play the whore. The fire which dissolved the body of even a Hercules enjoyed the supper, and the altar consumed everything. Larentina sleeps alone in the temple; and *she* a woman from the brothel, boasts that in her dreams she had submitted herself to the pleasure of Hercules; and she might possibly have experienced this, as it passed through her mind, in her sleep. In the morning, on going out of the temple very early, she is solicited by a young man—"a third Hercules," so to speak. He invites her home. She complies, remembering that Hercules had told her that it would be for her advantage. He then, to be sure, obtains permission that they should be united in lawful wedlock (for none was allowed to have intercourse with the concubine of a god without being punished for it); the husband makes her his heir. By and by, just before her death, she bequeathed to the Roman people the rather large estate

Ad Nationes

which she had obtained through Hercules. After this she sought deification for her daughters too, whom indeed the divine Larentina ought to have appointed her heirs also. The gods of the Romans received an accession in her dignity. For she alone of all the wives of Hercules was dear to him, because she alone was rich; and she was even far more fortunate than Ceres, who contributed to the pleasure of the (king of the) dead. After so many examples and *eminent* names among you, who might not have been declared divine? Who, in fact, ever raised a question as to his divinity against Antinous? Was even Ganymede more grateful and dear than he to (the supreme god) who loved him? According to you, heaven is open to the dead. You prepare a way from Hades to the stars. Prostitutes mount it in all directions, so that you must not suppose that you are conferring a great distinction upon your kings.

Chapter XI.—The Romans Provided Gods for Birth, Nay, Even Before Birth, to Death. Much Indelicacy in This System.

And you are not content to assert the divinity of such as were once known to you, whom you heard and handled, and whose portraits have been painted, and actions recounted, and memory retained amongst you; but men insist upon consecrating with a heavenly life I know not what incorporeal, inanimate shadows, and the *mere* names of things—dividing man's entire existence amongst separate powers even from his conception in the womb: so that there is a god Consevius, to preside over concubital generation; and Fluviona, to preserve the (growth of the) infant in the womb; after these come Vitumnus and Sentinus, through whom the babe begins to have life and its earliest sensation; then Diespiter, by whose office the child accomplishes its birth. But when women begin their parturition, Candelifera also *comes in* aid, since childbearing requires the light of the candle; and other goddesses there are[958] who get their names from the parts they bear in the stages of travail. There were two Carmentas likewise, according to the general view: to one of them, called Postverta, belonged the function of assisting the birth of the introverted child; while the other, Prosa, executed the like office for the rightly born. The god Farinus was so called from (his inspiring) the first utterance; while others believed in Locutius from his gift of speech. Cunina is present as the protector of the child's deep slumber, and supplies to it refreshing rest. To lift them (when fallen) there is Levana, and along with her Rumina. It is a wonderful oversight that no gods were appointed for cleaning up the filth of children. Then, to preside over their first pap and earliest drink you have Potina and Edula; to teach the child to stand erect is the work of Statina, whilst Adeona helps him to come to *dear Mamma*, and Abeona to toddle off again; then there is Domiduca, (to bring home the bride;) and the goddess Mens, to influence the mind to either good or evil. They have likewise Volumnus and Voleta, to control the will; Paventina, (the goddess) of fear; Venilia, of hope; Volupia, of pleasure; Præstitia, of beauty. Then, again, they give his name to Peragenor, from his teaching men to go through their work; to Consus, from his suggesting to them counsel. Juventa is their guide on assuming the manly gown, and "bearded Fortune" when they come to full manhood. If I must touch on their nuptial duties, there is Afferenda whose appointed function is to see to the offering of the dower; but fie on you! you have your Mutunus and Tutunus and Pertunda and Subigus and the goddess Prema and likewise Perfica. O spare yourselves, ye impudent gods! No one is present at the secret struggles of married life. Those very few persons who have a wish that way, go away and blush for very shame in the midst of their joy.

Chapter XII.—The Original Deities Were Human—With Some Very Questionable Characteristics. Saturn or Time Was Human. Inconsistencies of Opinion About Him.

Now, how much further need I go in recounting your gods—because I want to descant on the character of such as you have adopted? It is quite uncertain whether I shall laugh at your absurdity, or upbraid you for your blindness. For how many, and indeed what, gods shall I bring forward? Shall it be the greater ones, or the lesser? The old ones, or the novel? The male, or the female? The unmarried, or such as are joined in wedlock? The clever, or the unskillful? The rustic or the town ones? The national or the foreign? For the truth is, there are so many families, so many nations, which require a catalogue (of gods), that they cannot possibly be examined, or distinguished, or described. But the more diffuse the subject is, the more restriction must we impose on it. As, therefore, in this review we keep before us but one object—that of proving that all these gods were once human beings (not, indeed, to instruct you in the fact, for your conduct shows that you have forgotten it)—let us adopt our compendious summary from the most natural method of conducting the examination, even by considering the origin of their race. For the origin characterizes all that comes after it. Now this origin of your gods dates, I suppose, from Saturn. And when Varro mentions Jupiter, Juno, and Minerva, as the most ancient of the gods, it ought not to have escaped our notice, that every father is more ancient than his sons, and that Saturn therefore must precede Jupiter, even as Coelus does Saturn, for Saturn was sprung from Coelus and Terra. I pass by, however, the origin of Coelus and Terra. They led in some unaccountable way single lives, and had no children. Of course they required a long time for vigorous growth to attain to such a stature. By and by, as soon as the voice of Coelus began to break, and the breasts of Terra to become firm, they contract marriage with one another. I suppose either Heaven came down to his spouse, or Earth went up to meet her lord. Be that as it may, Earth conceived seed of Heaven, and when her year was fulfilled brought forth Saturn in a wonderful manner. Which of his parents did he resemble? Well, then, even after parentage began, it is certain that they had no child previous to Saturn, and only one daughter afterwards—Ops; thenceforth they ceased to procreate. The truth is, Saturn castrated Coelus as he was sleeping. We read this name Coelus as of the masculine gender. And for the matter of that, how could he be a father unless he were a male? But with what instrument was the castration effected? He had a scythe. What, so early as that? For Vulcan was not yet an artificer in iron. The widowed Terra, however, although still quite young, was in no hurry to marry another. Indeed, there was no second Coelus for her. What but Ocean offers her an embrace? But he savors of brackishness, and she has been accustomed to fresh water. And so Saturn is the sole male child of Coelus and Terra. When grown to puberty, he marries his own sister. No laws as yet prohibited incest, nor punished parricide. Then, when male children were born to him, he would devour them; better himself (should take them) than the wolves, (for to these would they become a prey) if he exposed them. He was, no doubt, afraid that one of them might learn the lesson of his father's scythe. When Jupiter was born in course of time, he was removed out of the way: (the father) swallowed a stone instead of the son, as was pretended. This artifice secured his safety for a time; but at length the son, whom he had not devoured, and who had grown up in secret, fell upon him, and deprived him of his kingdom. Such, then, is the patriarch of the gods whom Heaven and Earth produced for you, with the poets officiating as midwives. Now some persons with a refined imagination are of opinion that, by this allegorical fable of Saturn, there is a physiological representation of *Time*: (they think) that it is because all things are destroyed by Time, that Coelus and Terra were themselves parents without having any of their own, and that the (fatal) scythe was used, and that (Saturn) devoured his own offspring, because he, in fact, absorbs within himself all things which have issued from him. They call in also the witness of his

name; for they say that he is called Κρόνος in Greek, meaning

the same thing as χρόνος. His Latin name also they derive from

seed-sowing; for they suppose him to have been the actual procreator—that the seed, in fact, was dropt down from heaven to earth by his means. They unite him with *Ops*, because seeds produce the affluent treasure (*Opem*) of actual life, and because they develop with labor (*Opus*). Now I wish that you would explain this metaphorical statement. It was either Saturn or Time. If it was Time, how could it be Saturn? If he, how could it be Time? For you cannot possibly reckon both these corporeal subjects as co-existing in one person. What, however, was there to prevent your worshipping Time under its proper quality? Why not make a human person, or even a mythic man, an object of your adoration, but each in its proper nature not in the character of Time? What is the meaning of that conceit of your mental ingenuity, if it be not to color the foulest matters with the feigned appearance of reasonable proofs? Neither, on the one hand, do you mean Saturn to be Time, because you say he is a human being; nor, on the other hand, whilst portraying him as Time, do you on that account mean that he was ever human. No doubt, in the accounts of remote antiquity your god Saturn is plainly described as living on earth in human guise. Anything whatever may obviously be pictured as incorporeal which never had an existence; there is simply no room for such fiction, where there is reality. Since, therefore, there is clear evidence that Saturn once existed, it is in vain that you change his character. He whom you will not deny to have once been man, is not at your disposal to be treated anyhow, nor can it be maintained that he is either divine or Time. In every page of your literature the origin of Saturn is conspicuous. We read of him in Cassius Severus and in the Corneliuses, Nepos and Tacitus, and, amongst the Greeks also, in Diodorus, and all other compilers of ancient annals. No more faithful records of him are to be traced than in Italy itself. For, after (traversing) many countries, and (enjoying) the hospitality of Athens, he settled in Italy, or, as it was called, OEnotria, having met with a kind welcome from Janus, or Janes, as the Salii call him. The hill on which he settled had the name Saturnius, whilst the city which he founded still bears the name Saturnia; in short, the whole of Italy once had the same designation. Such is the testimony derived from that country which is now the mistress of the world: whatever doubt prevails about the origin of Saturn, his actions tell us plainly that he was a human being. Since, therefore, Saturn was human, he came undoubtedly from a human stock; and more, because he was a man, he, of course, came not of Coelus and Terra. Some people, however, found it easy enough to call him, whose parents were unknown, the son of those gods from whom all may in a sense seem to be derived. For who is there that does not speak under a feeling of reverence of the heaven and the earth as his own father and mother? Or, in accordance with a custom amongst men, which induces them to say of any who are unknown or suddenly apparent, that "they came from the sky?" Hence it happened that, because a stranger appeared suddenly everywhere, it became the custom to call him a heaven-born man,—just as we also commonly call earth-born all those whose descent is unknown. I say nothing of the fact that such was the state of antiquity, when men's eyes and minds were so habitually rude, that they were excited by the appearance of every newcomer as if it were that of a god: much more would this be the case with a king, and that the primeval one. I will linger some time longer over the case of Saturn, because by fully discussing his primordial history I shall beforehand furnish a compendious answer for all other cases; and I do not wish to omit the more convincing testimony of your sacred literature, the credit of which ought to be the greater in proportion to its antiquity. Now earlier than all literature was the Sibyl; that Sibyl, I mean, who was the true prophetess of truth, from whom you borrow their title for the priests of your demons. She in senarian verse expounds the descent of Saturn and his exploits in words to this effect: "In the tenth generation of men, after the flood had overwhelmed the former race, reigned Saturn, and Titan, and Japetus, the bravest of the sons of Terra and Coelus." Whatever credit, therefore, is attached to your older writers and literature, and much more to those who were the simplest as belonging to that age, it becomes sufficiently certain that Saturn and his family were human beings. We have in our possession, then, a brief principle which amounts to a prescriptive rule about their origin serving for all other cases, to prevent our going wrong in individual instances. The particular character of a posterity is shown by the original founders of the race—mortal beings (come) from mortals, earthly ones from earthly; step after step comes in due relation—marriage, conception, birth—country, settlements, kingdoms, all give the clearest proofs. They, therefore who cannot deny the birth of men, must also admit their death; they who allow their mortality must not suppose them to be gods.

Chapter XIII.—The Gods Human at First. Who Had the Authority to Make Them Divine? Jupiter Not Only Human, But Immoral.

Manifest cases, indeed, like these have a force peculiarly their own. Men like Varro and his fellow-dreamers admit into the ranks of the divinity those whom they cannot assert to have been in their primitive condition anything but men; (and this they do) by affirming that they became gods after their death. Here, then, I take my stand. If your gods were elected to this dignity and deity, just as you recruit the ranks of your senate, you cannot help conceding, in your wisdom, that there must be someone supreme sovereign who has the power of selecting, and is a kind of Cæsar; and nobody is able to confer on others a thing over which he has not absolute control. Besides, if they were able to make gods of themselves after their death, pray tell me why they chose to be in an inferior condition at first? Or, again, if there is no one who made them gods, how can they be said to have been made such, if they could only have been made by someone else? There is therefore no ground afforded you for denying that there is a certain wholesale distributor of divinity. Let us accordingly examine the reasons for dispatching mortal beings to heaven. I suppose you will produce a pair of them. Whoever, then, is the awarder (of the divine honors), exercises his function, either that he may have some supports, or defenses, or it may be even ornaments to his own dignity; or from the pressing claims of the meritorious, that he may reward all the deserving. No other cause is it permitted us to conjecture. Now there is no one who, when bestowing a gift on another, does not act with a view to his own interest or the other's. This conduct, however, cannot be worthy of the Divine Being, inasmuch as His power is so great that He can make gods outright; whilst His bringing man into such request, on the pretence that he requires the aid and support of certain, even dead persons, is a strange conceit, since He was able from the very first to create for Himself immortal beings. He who has compared human things with divine will require no further arguments on these points. And yet the latter opinion ought to be discussed, that God conferred divine honors in consideration of meritorious claims. Well, then, if the award was made on such grounds, if heaven was opened to men of the primitive age because of their deserts, we must reflect that after that time no one was worthy of such honor; except it be, that there is now no longer such a place for anyone to attain to. Let us grant that anciently men may have deserved heaven by reason of their great merits. Then let us consider whether there really was such merit. Let the man who alleges that it did exist declare his own view of merit. Since the actions of men done in the very infancy of time are a valid claim for their deification, you consistently admitted to the honor the brother and sister who were stained with the sin of incest—Ops and Saturn. Your Jupiter too, stolen in his infancy, was unworthy of both the home and the nutriment accorded to human beings; and, as he deserved for so bad a child, he had to live in Crete. Afterwards, when full-grown, he dethrones his own father, who, whatever his parental character may have been, was most prosperous in his reign, king as he was of the golden age. Under him, a stranger to toil and want, peace maintained its joyous and gentle sway; under him— "Nulli subigebant arva coloni;" "No swains would bring the fields beneath their sway;" and without the importunity of any one the earth would bear all crops spontaneously. But he hated a father who had been guilty of incest, and had once mutilated his grandfather. And yet, behold, he himself marries his own sister; so that I should suppose the old adage was made for him:

Τοῦ πατρὸς τὸ παιδίον—"Father's own child." There was "not

a pin to choose" between the father's piety and the son's. If the laws had been just even at that early time, Jupiter ought to have been "sewed up in both sacks." After this corroboration of his lust with incestuous gratification, why should he hesitate to indulge himself lavishly in the lighter excesses of adultery and debauchery? Ever since poetry sported thus with his character, in some such way as is usual when a runaway slave is posted up in public, we have been in the habit of gossiping without restraint of his tricks in our chat with passers-by; sometimes sketching him out in the form of the very money which was the fee of his debauchery—as when (he personated) a bull, or rather paid the money's worth of one, and showered (gold) into the maiden's chamber, or rather forced his way in with a bribe; sometimes (figuring him) in the very likenesses of the parts which were acted—as the eagle which ravished (the beautiful youth), and the swan which sang (the enchanting song). Well now, are not such fables as these made up of the most disgusting intrigues and the worst of scandals? or would not the morals and tempers of men be likely to become wanton from such examples? In what manner demons, the offspring of evil angels who have been long engaged in their mission, have labored to turn men aside from the faith to unbelief and to such fables, we must not in this place speak of to any extent. As indeed the general body (of your gods), which took their cue from their kings, and princes, and instructors, was not of the self-same nature, it was in some other way that similarity of character was exacted by their authority. But how much the worst of them was he who (ought to have been, but) was not, the best of them? By a title peculiar to him, you are indeed in the habit of calling Jupiter "the Best," whilst in Virgil he is "Æquus Jupiter." All therefore were *like* him—incestuous towards their own kith and kin, unchaste to strangers, impious, unjust! Now he whom mythic story left untainted with no conspicuous infamy, was not worthy to be made a god.

Chapter XIV.—Gods, Those Which Were Confessedly Elevated to the Divine Condition, What Pre-Eminent Right Had They to Such Honor? Hercules an Inferior Character.

But since they will have it that those who have been admitted from the human state to the honors of deification should be kept separate from others, and that the distinction which Dionysius the Stoic drew should be made between the native and the factitious gods, I will add a few words concerning this last class also. I will take Hercules himself for raising the gist of a reply (to the question) whether he deserved heaven and divine honors? For, as men choose to have it, these honors are awarded to him for his merits. If it was for his velour in destroying wild beasts with intrepidity, what was there in that so very memorable? Do not criminals condemned to the games, though they are even consigned to the contest of the vile arena, dispatch several of these animals at one time, and that with more earnest zeal? If it was for his world-wide travels, how often has the same thing been accomplished by the rich at their pleasant leisure, or by philosophers in their slave-like poverty? Is it forgotten that the cynic Asclepiads on a single sorry cow, riding on her back, and sometimes nourished at her udder, surveyed the whole world with a personal inspection? Even if Hercules visited the infernal regions, who does not know that the way to Hades is open to all? If you have deified him on account of his much carnage and many battles, a much greater number of victories was gained by the illustrious Pompey, the conqueror of the pirates who had not spared Ostia itself in their ravages; and (as to carnage), how many thousands, let me ask, were cooped up in one corner of the citadel of Carthage, and slain by Scipio? Wherefore Scipio has a better claim to be considered a fit candidate for deification than Hercules. You must be still more careful to add to the claims of (our) Hercules his debaucheries with concubines *and* wives, and the swathes of Omphale, and his base desertion of the Argonauts because he had lost his beautiful boy. To this mark of baseness add for his glorification likewise his attacks of madness, adore the arrows which slew his sons and wife. This was the man who, after deeming himself worthy of a funeral pile in the anguish of his remorse for his parricides, deserved rather to die the unhonored death which awaited him, arrayed in the poisoned robe which his wife sent him on account of his lascivious attachment (to another). You, however, raised him from the pyre to the sky, with the same facility with which (you have distinguished in like manner) another hero also, who was destroyed by the violence of a fire from the gods. He having devised some few experiments, was said to have restored the dead to life by his cures. He was the son of Apollo, half human, although the grandson of Jupiter, and great-grandson of Saturn (or rather of spurious origin, because his parentage was uncertain, as Socrates of Argon has related; he was exposed also, and found in a worse tutelage than even Jove's, suckled even at the dugs of a dog); nobody can deny that he deserved the end which befell him when he perished by a stroke of lightning. In this transaction, however, your most excellent Jupiter is once more found in the wrong—impious to his grandson, envious of his artistic skill. Pindar, indeed, has not concealed his true desert; according to him, he was punished for his avarice and love of gain, influenced by which he would bring the living to their death, rather than the dead to life, by the perverted use of his medical art which he put up for sale. It is said that his mother was killed by the same stroke, and it was only right that she, who had bestowed so dangerous a beast on the world, should escape to heaven by the same ladder. And yet the Athenians will not be at a loss how to sacrifice to gods of such a fashion, for they pay divine honors to Æsculapius and his mother amongst their dead (worthies). As if, too, they had not ready to hand their own Theseus to worship, so highly deserving a god's distinction! Well, why not? Did he not on a foreign shore abandon the preserver of his life, with the same indifference, nay heartlessness, with which he became the cause of his father's death?

Chapter XV.—The Constellations and the Genii Very Indifferent Gods. The Roman Monopoly of Gods Unsatisfactory. Other Nations Require Deities Quite as Much.

It would be tedious to take a survey of all those, too, whom you have buried amongst the constellations, and audaciously minister to as gods. I suppose your Castors, and Perseus, and Erigona, have just the same claims for the honors of the sky as Jupiter's own big boy had. But why should we wonder? You have transferred to heaven even dogs, and scorpions, and crabs. I postpone all remarks concerning those whom you worship in your oracles. That this worship exists, is attested by him who pronounces the oracle. Why; you will have your gods to be spectators even of sadness, as is Viduus, who makes a *widow* of the soul, by parting it from the body, and whom you have condemned, by not permitting him to be enclosed within your city-walls; there is Cæculus also, to deprive the eyes of their perception; and Orbana, to bereave seed of its vital power; moreover, there is the goddess of death herself. To pass hastily by all others, you account as gods the sites of places or of the city; such are Father Janus (there being, moreover, the archer-goddess Jana), and Septimontius of the seven hills. Men sacrifice to the same *Genii*, whilst they have altars or temples in the same places; but to others besides, when they dwell in a strange place, or live in rented houses. I say nothing about Ascensus, who gets his name for his *climbing* propensity, and Clivicola, from her sloping (haunts); I pass silently by the deities called Forculus from doors, and Cardea from hinges, and Limentinus the god of thresholds, and whatever others are worshipped by your neighbors as tutelar deities of their street doors. There is nothing strange in this, since men have their respective gods in their brothels, their kitchens, and even in their prison. Heaven, therefore, is crowded with innumerable gods of its own, both these and others belonging to the Romans, which have distributed amongst them the functions of one's whole life, in such a way that there is no want of the other gods. Although, it is true, the gods which we have enumerated are reckoned as Roman peculiarly, and as not easily recognized abroad; yet how do all those functions and circumstances, over which men have willed their gods to preside, come about, in every part of the human race, and in every nation, where their guarantees are not only without an official recognition, but even any recognition at all?

Chapter XVI.—Inventors of Useful Arts Unworthy of Deification. They Would Be the First to Acknowledge a Creator. The Arts Changeable from Time to Time, and Some Become Obsolete.

Well, but certain men have discovered fruits and sundry necessaries of life, (and hence are worthy of deification). Now let me ask, when you call these persons "discoverers," do you not confess that what they discovered was already in existence? Why then do you not prefer to honor the Author, from whom the gifts really come, instead of converting the Author into *mere* discoverers? Previously he who made the discover, the inventor himself no doubt expressed his gratitude to the Author; no doubt, too, he felt that He was God, to whom really belonged the religious service, as the Creator (of the gift), by whom also both he who discovered and that which was discovered were alike created. The green fig of Africa nobody at Rome had heard of when Cato introduced it to the Senate, in order that he might show how near was that province of the enemy whose subjugation he was constantly urging. The cherry was first made common in Italy by Cn. Pompey, who imported it from Pontus. I might possibly have thought the earliest introducers of apples amongst the Romans deserving of the public honor of deification. This, however, would be as foolish a ground for making gods as even the invention of the useful arts. And yet if the skilful men of our own time be compared with these, how much more suitable would deification be to the later generation than to the former! For, tell me, have not all the extant inventions superseded antiquity, whilst daily experience goes on adding to the new stock? Those, therefore, whom you regard as divine because of their arts, you are really injuring by your very arts, and challenging (their divinity) by means of rival attainments, which cannot be surpassed.

Chapter XVII.—Conclusion, the Romans Owe Not Their Imperial Power to Their Gods. The Great God Alone Dispenses Kingdoms, He is the God of the Christians.

In conclusion, without denying all those whom antiquity willed *and* posterity has believed to be gods, to be the guardians of your religion, there yet remains for our consideration that very large assumption of the Roman superstitions which we have to meet in opposition to you, O heathen, viz. that the Romans have become the lords and masters of the whole world, because by their religious offices they have merited this dominion to such an extent that they are within a very little of excelling even their own gods in power. One cannot wonder that Sterculus, and Mutunus, and Larentina, have severally advanced this empire to its height! The Roman people has been by its gods alone ordained to such dominion. For I could not imagine that any foreign *gods* would have preferred doing more for a strange nation than for their own people, and so by such conduct become the deserters and neglecters, nay, the betrayers of the native land wherein they were born and bred, and ennobled and buried. Thus not even Jupiter could suffer his own Crete to be subdued by the Roman fasces, forgetting that cave of Ida, and the brazen cymbals of the Corybantes, and the most pleasant odor of *the goat* which nursed him on that *dear* spot. Would he not have made that tomb of his superior to the whole Capitol, so that that land should most widely rule which covered the ashes of Jupiter? Would Juno, *too*, be willing that the Punic city, for the love of which she even neglected Samos, should be destroyed, and that, too, by the fires of the sons of Æneas?
Although I am well aware that

"Hic illius arma,
   Hic currus fuit, hoc regnum des gentibus esse,
   Si qua fata sinant, jam tunc tenditque fovetque."
   "Here were her arms, her chariot here,
   Here goddess-like, to fix one day
   The seat of universal sway,
   Might fate be wrung to yield assent,
   E'en then her schemes, her cares were bent."

Still the unhappy (queen of gods) had no power against the fates! And yet the Romans did not accord as much honor to the fates, although they gave them Carthage, as they did to Larentina. But surely those gods of yours have not the power of conferring empire. For when Jupiter reigned in Crete, and Saturn in Italy, and Isis in Egypt, it was even as men that they reigned, to whom also were assigned many to assist them. Thus he who serves also makes masters, and the bond-slave of Admetus aggrandizes with empire the citizens of Rome, although he destroyed his own liberal votary Croesus by deceiving him with ambiguous oracles. Being a god, why was he afraid boldly to foretell to him the truth that he must lose his kingdom. Surely those who were aggrandized with the power of wielding empire might always have been able to keep an eye, as it were, on their own cities. If they were strong enough to confer empire on the Romans, why did not Minerva defend Athens from Xerxes? Or why did not Apollo rescue Delphi out of the hand of Pyrrhus? They who lost their own cities preserve the city of Rome, since (forsooth) the religiousness of Rome has merited the protection! But is it not rather the fact that this excessive devotion has been devised since the empire has attained its glory by the increase of its power? No doubt sacred rites were introduced by Numa, but then your proceedings were not marred by a religion of idols and temples. Piety was simple, and worship humble; altars were artlessly reared, and the vessels (thereof) plain, and the incense from them scant, and the god himself nowhere. Men therefore were not religious before they achieved greatness, (nor great) because they were religious. But how can the Romans possibly seem to have acquired their empire by an excessive religiousness and very profound respect for the gods, when that empire was rather increased after the gods had been slighted? Now, if I am not mistaken, every kingdom or empire is acquired and enlarged by wars, whilst they and their gods also are injured by conquerors. For the same ruin affects both city-walls and temples; similar is the carnage both of civilians and of priests; identical the plunder of profane things and of sacred. To the Romans belong as many sacrileges as trophies; and then as many triumphs over gods as over nations. Still remaining are their captive idols amongst them; and certainly, if they can only see their conquerors, they do not give them their love. Since, however, they have no perception, they are injured with impunity; and since they are injured with impunity, they are worshipped to no purpose. The nation, therefore, which has grown to its powerful height by victory after victory, cannot seem to have developed owing to the merits of its religion—whether they have injured the religion by augmenting their power, or augmented their power by injuring the religion. All nations have possessed empire, each in its proper time, as the Assyrians, the Medes, the Persians, the Egyptians; empire is even now also in the possession of some, and yet they that have lost their power used not to behave without attention to religious services and the worship of the gods, even after these had become unpropitious to them, until at last almost universal dominion has accrued to the Romans. It is the fortune of the times that has thus constantly shaken kingdoms with revolution. Inquire who has ordained these changes in the times. It is the same (great Being) who dispenses kingdoms, and has now put the supremacy of them into the hands of the Romans, very much as if the tribute of many nations were after its exaction amassed in one (vast) coffer. What He has determined concerning it, they know who are the nearest to Him.

Appendix.

A Fragment Concerning the Execrable Gods of the Heathen.

So great blindness has fallen on the Roman race, that they call their enemy Lord, and preach the filcher of blessings as being their very giver, and to him they give thanks. They call those (deities), then, by human names, not by their own, for their own names they know not. That they are dæmons they understand: but they read histories of the old kings, and then, though they see that their character was mortal, they honor them with a deific name.

As for him whom they call Jupiter, and think to be the highest god, when he was born the years (that had elapsed) from the foundation of the world to him were some three thousand. He is born in Greece, from Saturnus and Ops; and, for fear he should be killed by his father (or else, if it is lawful to say so, should be begotten anew), is by the advice of his mother carried down into Crete, and reared in a cave of Ida; is concealed from his father's search) by (the aid of) Cretans—born men!—rattling their arms; sucks a she-goat's dugs; flays her; clothes himself in her hide; and (thus) uses his own nurse's hide, after killing her, to be sure, with his own hand! but he sewed thereon three golden tassels worth the price of an hundred oxen each, as their author Homer relates, if it is fair to believe it. This Jupiter, in adult age, waged war several years with his father; overcame him; made a parricidal raid on his home; violated his virgin sisters; selected one of them in marriage; drave his father by dint of arms. The remaining scenes, moreover, of that act have been recorded. Of other folks' wives, or else of violated virgins, he begat him sons; defiled freeborn boys; oppressed peoples lawlessly with despotic and kingly sway. The father, whom they erringly suppose to have been the *original* god, was ignorant that this (son of his) was lying concealed in Crete; the son, again, whom they believe the *mightier* god, knows not that the father whom himself had banished is lurking in Italy. If he was in heaven, when would he not see what was doing in Italy? For the Italian land is "not in a corner." And yet, had he been a god, nothing *ought* to have escaped him. But that he whom the Italians call Saturnus did lurk there, is clearly evidenced on the face of it, from the fact that from his lurking the Hesperian tongue is to this day called Latin, as likewise their author Virgil relates.(Jupiter,) then, is said to have been born on earth, while (Saturnus his father) fears lest he be driven by him from his kingdom, and seeks to kill him as being his own rival, and knows not that he has been stealthily carried off, and is in hiding; and afterwards the son-god pursues his father, immortal seeks to slay immortal (is it credible?), and is disappointed by an interval of sea, and is ignorant of (his quarry's) flight; and while all this is going on between two gods on earth, heaven is deserted. No one dispensed the rains, no one thundered, no one governed all this mass of world. For they cannot even say that their action and wars took place in heaven; for all this was going on on Mount Olympus in Greece. Well, but heaven is not called Olympus, for heaven is heaven.

These, then, are the actions of theirs, which we will treat of first—nativity, lurking, ignorance, parricide, adulteries, obscenities—things committed not by a god, but by most impure and truculent human beings; beings who, had they been living in these days, would have lain under the impeachment of all laws—laws which are far more just and strict than *their* actions. "He drave his father by dint of arms." The Falcidian and Sempronian law would bind the parricide in a sack with beasts. "He violated his sisters." The Papinian law would punish the outrage with all penalties, limb by limb. "He invaded others' wedlock." The Julian law would visit its adulterous violator capitally. "He defiled freeborn boys." The Cornelian law would condemn the crime of transgressing the sexual bond with novel severities, sacrilegiously guilty as it is of a novel union. This being is shown to have had no divinity either, for he was a human being; his father's flight escaped him. To this human being, of such a character, to so wicked a king, so obscene and so cruel, God's honor has been assigned by men. Now, to be sure, if *on earth* he were born and grew up through the advancing stages of life's periods, and in it committed all these evils, and yet is no more in it, what is thought (of him) but that he is dead? Or else does foolish error think wings were born him in his old age, whence to fly heavenward? Why, even *this* may possibly find credit among men bereft of sense, if indeed they believe, (as they do,) that he turned into a swan, to beget the Castors; an eagle, to contaminate Ganymede; a bull, to violate Europa; gold, to violate Danaë; a horse, to beget Pirithoüs; a goat, to beget Egyppa from a she-goat; a Satyr, to embrace Antiope. Beholding these adulteries, to which sinners are prone, they therefore easily believe that sanctions of misdeed and of every filthiness are borrowed from their feigned god. Do they perceive how void of amendment are the rest of his career's acts which can find credit, which are indeed true, and which, they say, he did without self transformation? Of Semele, he begets Liber; of Latona, Apollo and Diana; of Maia, Mercury; of Alcmena, Hercules. But the rest of his corruptions, which they themselves confess, I am unwilling to record, lest turpitude, once buried, be again called to men's ears. But of these few (offspring of his) I have made mention; off-springs whom in their error they believe to be themselves, too, gods—born, to wit, of an incestuous father; adulterous births, supposititious births. And the living, eternal God, of sempiternal divinity, prescient of futurity, immeasurable, they have dissipated (into nothing, by associating Him) with crimes so unspeakable.

Elucidation.
———————

This Fragment is noted as spurious, by Oehler who attributes it to somebody only moderately acquainted with Tertullian's style and teaching. I do not find it mentioned by Dupin, nor by Routh. This translation is by Thelwall.

Made in the USA
San Bernardino, CA
26 September 2016